A VISION FOR CONVERSION

A Vision
for Conversion

Eight Steps to Radically Change Your RCIA Process

Leisa Anslinger

LITURGICAL PRESS

Collegeville, Minnesota

www.litpress.org

Library of Congress Cataloging-in-Publication Data

Names: Anslinger, Leisa, author. | Catholic Church. Ordo initiationis Christianae adultorum. English
Title: A vision for conversion : eight steps to radically change your RCIA process / Leisa Anslinger.
Description: Collegeville, Minnesota : Liturgical Press, [2018] | Series: TeamRCIA | Includes bibliographical references.
Identifiers: LCCN 2018017574 (print) | LCCN 2018034324 (ebook) | ISBN 9780814644409 (ebook) | ISBN 9780814644157
Subjects: LCSH: Catholic Church. Ordo initiationis Christianae adultorum. | Initiation rites—Religious aspects—Catholic Church—Study and teaching. | Catechetics—Catholic Church—Study and teaching.
Classification: LCC BX2045.I553 (ebook) | LCC BX2045.I553 A57 2018 (print) | DDC 264/.020813--dc23
LC record available at https://lccn.loc.gov/2018017574.

Contents

Introduction

Propelling People and the Parish toward Living Discipleship

My first year as an RCIA coordinator was more than I could have imagined it might be and occasionally felt like more than I could manage. There always seemed to be something that needed my attention, from forming a team to responding to the people who expressed interest in participating. Discerning who would speak to various topics and do so from spiritual depth and a firm grasp of Catholic teaching was especially important in that first year, as was the development of a year-round process, which we had not previously attempted at our parish. I remember graced conversations with early participants and the sense of responsibility in ensuring that the process would form them as committed disciples of Jesus Christ. I recall specific RCIA sessions, ones where the process fell flat, and others that seemed particularly filled with the Holy Spirit. I especially recall the Easter Vigil, the flood of emotions, prayers for the newly initiated, and the hope that this was the beginning of a lifetime of faith for them and their families.

Throughout the year, I saw faith come to life among the participants and looked forward to Sunday dismissals and Thursday evening sessions. With all of the time and attention on the participants in that first year, I have to admit I was not quite prepared for the impact of the process on myself and the RCIA team. Nor did I anticipate the ways in which the participants in the RCIA process (the inquirers, catechumens, and candidates) would touch the wider parish community. Beginning with the Rite of Acceptance into the Order of Catechumens and regular dismissal from the Sunday assembly, our team heard how the presence of the catechumens among the community called people to examine their own commitment to Christ. I experienced firsthand the interaction of participants and parishioners that the RCIA describes:

> The period of postbaptismal catechesis is of great significance for both the neophytes and the rest of the faithful. Through it the neophytes, with the help of their godparents, should experience a full and joyful welcome into the community and enter into closer ties with the other faithful. The faithful, in turn, should derive from it a renewal of inspiration and of outlook. (246)

The RCIA propelled participants, the team, and the whole parish toward an encounter with Christ and to living discipleship.

It Is All about Change

It took many years for me to grasp that the RCIA, and all of the Christian life, is ultimately about change—following Jesus Christ is the work of a lifetime, and ongoing conversion necessarily requires change of mind, heart, life, and action. We are never finished products in the faith. Discipleship calls us to continual discernment, spiritually assessing how we might be called to live, grow, learn, serve, and love more deeply as Christ's Body in the world.

As people who accompany others toward initiation, we must guide them to embrace and manage change. The ways in which we carry out the RCIA process will have great bearing on how the participants navigate the various stages of the journey toward initiation and the Christian life. Not only this, as the RCIA team and participants embrace a life of ongoing conversion in Christ, we become catalysts for change within the parish toward the formation of a community that is committed to living discipleship.

Who Should Read This Book

Chances are, if you are perusing this book, it is for you! *A Vision for Conversion* is for all who are involved in RCIA ministry and in shaping parish life: pastors, RCIA coordinators and team members, staff members, pastoral councils, faith formation committees, and parish leadership teams. While you might read this book on your own, it would be especially appropriate to read it with others. The book is intended to equip you with the knowledge and skills necessary to be attentive to the dynamics of change and to lead for it—spiritual change as people embrace a life of conversion to Christ and change within the parish as a community that is committed to lead people to living discipleship. Questions for reflection and discussion are included at the end of each chapter to guide conversation and to help you discern future action.

A Vision for Conversion is written with the conviction that we are all servant leaders. Each of us—as members of Christ's body—is called to lead one another to Christ or more deeply to Christ. Each is called to serve; each is given particular gifts and talents with which to do so. The Holy Spirit enlivens, empowers, and strengthens us to carry out Christ's mission on earth. Those who have accepted an invitation to serve as an RCIA coordinator or team member, those who serve on the pastoral council or faith formation committee, all who serve in ministry within the parish and beyond it—each is a leader and has a role to play in contributing to the mission of Christ and the church.

Why You Should Read This Book

Accompanying people on the spiritual journey, especially RCIA participants, is a sacred responsibility. Pope Francis points to this in The Joy of the Gospel: "In our world, ordained ministers and other pastoral workers can make present the fragrance of Christ's closeness and his personal gaze. The Church will have to initiate everyone—priests, religious, and laity—into this 'art of accompaniment' which teaches us to remove our sandals before the sacred ground of the other" (169). Understanding the call of conversion as a process of change will help us to be prepared to stand on this sacred ground. For many, change is not easy. In fact, it can be frightening. It entails risk as we step into the unknown. While this is true in all facets of life, it is especially so in the spiritual life. Establishing an environment in which people are encouraged to embrace change as part of the journey of discipleship will give the RCIA team and participants the security needed to be open to conversion.

Additionally, the RCIA process is evangelizing. Studies of the Center for Applied Research in the Apostolate (CARA) demonstrate that those who participate in the RCIA are more likely to actively participate in Mass and the sacrament of reconciliation than those who were baptized as infants (see Mark M. Gray, ed., "How Many Catholic Converts Stay?"). Most pastors, staff members, and involved parishioners recognize those who have participated in the RCIA among their most active members. Their commitment to Christ and to discipleship is inspiring! As parishioners experience the enthusiasm of the RCIA participants and team, they are led to peer deeply into their own lives, experience, and commitment to Jesus Christ and to embrace conversion themselves. As people who are charged with leadership in the RCIA as coordinator or team members, or in shaping parish life as a pastor, staff person, or parishioner leader, it is imperative that we direct the RCIA for the greatest possible impact on participants and team members and enable the parish to be influenced and inspired by this vital process.

Eight Steps to Change

While change is not always easy, it is possible to guide people and the parish to not only manage it but to welcome it as a key aspect of the life of discipleship. Each chapter of *A Vision for Conversion* draws on one of eight steps of change that have been identified and explored in the work of Dr. John Kotter, professor emeritus of Harvard Business School and recognized authority on the dynamics and process of change. Kotter's work has previously been applied to the life of businesses, schools, and nonprofit groups with great benefit to these organizations. It may not immediately be apparent how a model that was developed for businesses and organizations would apply to the spiritual life of individuals or the parish. There is much that is applicable, however, and I am convinced that Kotter's eight steps, detailed and explored in *Leading Change*, are a helpful framework for ministry.

We will be going into all the details of how you can take each of these steps to make your RCIA process into a powerful conversion journey for your seekers, your RCIA team, and your whole parish. As a quick preview, these are the eight steps:

1. Establish a vision.

2. Create a vision team.

3. Make your vision a reality.

4. Share your vision.

5. Remove barriers to your vision.

6. Celebrate progress toward your vision.

7. Keep your vision alive.

8. Make your vision last.

With these steps in mind, we will be agents of change toward a dynamic, genuine life of ongoing conversion in Christ. "This is crucial: we must be converted—and we must continue to be converted! We must let the Holy Spirit change our lives! We must respond to Jesus Christ" (USCCB, Go and Make Disciples, 14).

Our Process

Each chapter begins with an exploration of the RCIA and the way the RCIA may influence the spiritual life of the parish. We will lay theological, spiritual, and pastoral foundations from which we will establish a compelling vision for the future. Particularly in the first three chapters, we will establish a vision and capture the need for change.

Following the section on the RCIA and the parish in each chapter, I will invite you to examine your own experience in relationship to the steps of change leadership toward a fuller and more faith-filled life for seekers, team members, and parishioners. Chapter 3 concludes with a process to help you identify and articulate what will be necessary in order to effect this change in the parish, including initial strategies to move toward the vision in the immediate future. In chapters 4 through 8, we will enhance the vision and outline the steps necessary to begin to enact the changes you have discerned.

We will use the Appreciative Inquiry (AI) method to create a simple and doable plan, initially at the end of chapter 3 and again at the end of the book. I will give you discussion questions to help you apply the steps of change leadership to implement the changes you discern within the spiritual lives of individuals, the RCIA process, and in the life of the parish.

Appreciative Inquiry provides a process through which you may consider your current practices and experience in relationship to your vision, mission, and goals, identifying areas in need of change. Throughout this book you will learn steps to bring about the changes you identify, and you will develop strategies to lead for that change. There are four steps of Appreciative Inquiry:

1. **Discover**: What is your current experience or practice? What is already working? What positively contributes to the dimension under consideration? What stories come to mind that capture this experience or practice?

2. **Dream**: What is your vision? What are your hopes, dreams, and goals for this dimension?

3. **Discern**: What should be? What needs to change in order to move from your current practice toward your vision?

4. **Do**: What will you do to bring about the change you have discerned?

Establish a Vision

The Vision: Answering Christ's Call

The RCIA is an evangelizing process drawing people deeply to the love of God in Jesus Christ through the Holy Spirit. In the RCIA, we accompany seekers through distinct periods of conversion. We help them to answer the Lord's call. As participants and team members respond to God's grace and give witness to the power of faith in their lives, the entire community is inspired to do the same. "Jesus' call is urgent. He does not tell people to follow him at some time in the future but here and now—at *this* moment, in *these* circumstances. There can be no delay. 'Go and proclaim the kingdom of God . . . No one who sets a hand to the plow and looks to what was left behind is fit for the kingdom of God' (Luke 9:60, 62)" (USCCB, Stewardship: A Disciple's Response, 14). This urgent call of Christ is the reason, goal, and meaning of our ministry; in fact, it is the purpose of our entire life. Discerning how we will respond to the call of Christ at this moment, in these circumstances, personally, within the RCIA team, among participants, and in the parish, determines what takes priority; where we will spend energy; what needs to change, and why.

Reflection attributed to Pedro Arrupe, SJ

Nothing is more practical than
finding God, than
falling in Love
in a quite absolute, final way.
What you are in love with,
what seizes your imagination, will affect everything.
It will decide
what will get you out of bed in the morning,
what you do with your evenings,
how you spend your weekends,
what you read, whom you know,
what breaks your heart,
and what amazes you with joy and gratitude.
Fall in Love, stay in love,
and it will decide everything.

Change: Why?

Why explore and apply principles of change to the ways in which we accompany RCIA participants through the initiation process? Why consider the relationship between the RCIA and the life of the parish? These questions are fundamental to our approach throughout this book and the process we will explore here. It is not enough to say that change is important. We must accept that change is necessary. More than this. We must be convinced that change is desirable—our end goal that is never fully accomplished. We must be ready to be catalysts of change if people and the parish are to be transformed.

The question of why change is such a vital dimension of our pastoral life is simultaneously theological, spiritual, and practical:

- **Theological**: Our mission is to form disciples. We who have accepted Christ's call to evangelize and to serve recognize our role in leading others to the fullness of life in Christ, which, as we have already noted, is essentially a life of on-going conversion. This clear sense of mission is essential in the lives of individuals and the life (and sustainability) of the parish. We will explore this in greater depth throughout this book.

- **Spiritual**: The RCIA is aimed primarily at spiritual formation.

  The rite of Christian initiation presented here is designed for adults who, after hearing the mystery of Christ proclaimed, consciously and freely seek the living God and enter the way of faith and conversion as the Holy Spirit opens their hearts. By God's help they will be strengthened spiritually during their preparation and at the proper time will receive the sacraments fruitfully. (*Rite of Christian Initiation of Adults*, 1)

  We who are responsible for the RCIA and those who shape parish life will do well to be attentive to the spiritual life of participants and team members as well as the wider parish community. This, too, will receive our further attention.

- **Practical**: There are many practical concerns that make this a particularly crucial and timely topic. These practical things have spiritual implications, and the spiritual lives of people and the parish impact the practical factors below:

  - *Declining numbers of adults who are baptized or received into full communion*: The RCIA process is essential in forming those who are preparing for initiation, and those who are initiated as adults are much more likely to actively live their faith through participation in Mass and the sacrament of reconciliation. Yet, the number of adults who are baptized or received into full communion is steadily declining, as are the number of people receiving first Holy Communion, confirmation, and the sacrament of marriage (CARA).

  - *Increase in the number of former adult Catholics*: While the number of Catholics in the United States increases most years, the addition of people is largely due to immigration. "As the largest religion in the U.S., Catholicism has the largest number of former members (some later return as reverts)" (CARA, "Frequently Requested Church Statistics"). Catholicism is not alone in such a decline. In fact, identification with most religions is steadily declining. And while "Catholicism has a higher retention rate than most other religions in the U.S. (including all Protestant denominations)" (CARA), there is much cause for concern, as the impact of declining affiliation influences every aspect of the life of the parish and the church. We will explore this reality throughout this book as we consider the influence of the RCIA on the parish and the need for broader initiatives toward discipleship and ongoing conversion among all in the faith community.

- *The unaffiliated*: Related to the increase in the number of former Catholics is the recognition that many who were raised Catholic are no longer a member of any religious denomination. The fastest-growing religious "group" in the United States is the unaffiliated ("Faith in Flux," Pew Research Center), nicknamed the "nones" by sociologists because they answer "none" to survey questions regarding religious affiliation.

- *Declining participation in Mass*: Those who do remain Catholic participate in Sunday Mass less frequently than in previous decades. Current data indicates that about 22 percent of Catholics regularly attend Sunday Mass (CARA).

Fewer people are participating in Mass. Declining numbers of people are becoming Catholic. Larger numbers of people, especially younger adults, are leaving the practice of the faith. Why is change necessary? Do we even need to ask? All of these point to the need for individuals and communities that are alive and fervent in faith and are ready to share the Good News of Jesus Christ.

Think about your personal commitment as a disciple and about the life of your parish. Do you, does your parish, have a strong sense of mission? Can you capture that mission clearly and succinctly? How well are you and your parish fulfilling that mission at this point in time?

You may be experiencing some or all of the factors detailed above in your parish. Perhaps you have fewer RCIA participants each year, or you are concerned that Mass attendance is decreasing little by little. Each national statistic is made up of the experience of people and parishes just like yours. If your parish is not in decline, it is important to be attentive to what is contributing to the life and faith that you are experiencing. Build on that. Every parish and process has strengths upon which to build, as well as areas that need to be addressed. It is not enough to note the influence of the surrounding culture and the trends toward declining religiosity in the Western world. We are not good stewards of our faith by resigning ourselves to a gradual state of decline, nor are we responsible as people of ministry when we maintain the status quo even when we know that change is necessary and beneficial. Growth is always possible. The alternative is stagnation, decline, and failure to fulfill our mission as servant leaders and disciples of our Lord Jesus Christ.

We do not consider change for change's sake nor for the goal of increasing numbers. Rather, we lead for and manage change in order to fulfill the mission of Christ and the church. The church exists to evangelize, baptizing in the name of the Father, Son, and Holy Spirit, leading people to become more fully committed disciples who love and serve as followers of Jesus Christ.

We must be honest with ourselves and admit that there are many aspects of the life of the parish, including the RCIA, that would benefit from prayerful, pastoral examination. Such careful appraisal is sure to surface areas that are in need of change in order to carry out our mission, to more faithfully and fully lead people to a dynamic life of faith. "There are ecclesial structures which can hamper efforts at evangelization, yet even good structures are only helpful when there is a life constantly driving, sustaining, and assessing them. Without new life and an authentic evangelical spirit, without the Church's 'fidelity to her own calling,' any new structure will soon prove ineffective" (Joy of the Gospel, 26).

Change: Who?

Throughout *A Vision for Conversion*, we will explore three focus points, or subjects, of change:

People: The RCIA Participants and Team

Those who are spiritually committed are rooted in a life of prayer and participation in the faith community, responsive to God's grace, and continually discern their vocation—who they are called to be, and what they are called to do. RCIA coordinators, team members, and participants share a spiritual journey together. Not only do coordinators and team members accompany participants as they journey toward initiation, they support one another as they strive to live and grow as committed disciples. It is, therefore, beneficial to be aware of the dynamics of change and to lead toward a life of ongoing conversion among the RCIA team and participants.

Process: The RCIA Process as It Is Enacted in the Parish

The *Rite of Christian Initiation of Adults* is a process of spiritual and faith formation marked by specific liturgical rites at various stages of the journey toward initiation. The RCIA is carried out in local parish communities under the guidance of the local bishop and the pastor of the parish. There are many factors that contribute to the ways in which we respond to seekers, guide their spiritual and faith formation, and enact the liturgical rites. Examining the manner in which the RCIA is implemented in the parish is essential to its success in initiation ministry and in positively contributing to the spiritual life of the parish.

Parish: The Parish as a Faith Community of Disciples

The RCIA has the potential to evangelize the wider parish community. The more we lead parishioners to an encounter with our Lord and to respond to God's grace as disciples of Jesus Christ, the greater the possibility that the parish will grow as an "evangelizing community" (Joy of the Gospel, 24). The RCIA as a process of conversion inspires parishioners to be open and responsive to God's love, and that leads them to share their experience and enthusiasm with others in the daily circumstances of their lives.

These three groups, the people, the process, and the parish, are interrelated. When one remains static, the others are less likely to embrace conversion; when one is transformed, the others will be more likely to be led to renewal of faith and life.

Change: What and Why

What needs to change? Just as each person will experience and respond to the call to conversion in the daily circumstances of his or her life, each community would do well to discern the areas of parish life that are in need of change. Throughout this book, you will be encouraged to consider what needs to change and to intentionally lead for that change.

Leading for Change, Step 1: Establish Urgency

The first step of Kotter's change leadership framework is to establish a sense of urgency (37–52). In other words, why is change necessary? It may feel as though much of what we have explored up to this point in this book is preamble. It is actually part of step 1. Throughout all that has been stated up to now, we have been establishing our why. Why change is necessary. Why this topic has theological, spiritual, and practical implications with real-life impact for you, your RCIA participants, and your parish. Why it is imperative that we learn to lead for and manage change, and why it is up to you to be a catalyst for change.

Kotter points to complacency as the greatest obstacle to the process of change, particularly in this first step of establishing urgency. It is very easy for us to discount the need for change, saying aloud or thinking to ourselves, "it really isn't that bad," or "but the RCIA participants love the process as it is now," or "we just don't have time to deal with this right now. Things will be fine for a while longer." It is not until we are convinced that change is necessary that we will be committed to the process. Others will not embrace change without our leadership. Without a strong, clear sense of urgency, we will fall back into old patterns in the first moment of challenge or uncertainty.

Think about this from your own personal experience. I know how often I have told myself that something in my life needs to change. I need to pray more regularly or more attentively; my family needs more of my presence or attention; I need to eat healthier or exercise more. . . . You get the picture. I must admit, there have been times when I have resolved to change, whether at New Year's or the start of Lent. Much of the time, I begin the new practice and then slide back into old patterns. I tell myself I do not have the time, or I don't see the results I had hoped for, or I just lose steam. Sometimes, however, the change has become rooted in my life in such a way that it becomes habit. One year, our teenage daughter told me she had decided to eat a salad a day for the season of Lent. I decided to join her in the resolution. By the end of the forty days, salad had become part of my daily routine, from which I rarely stray, now over ten years later. My urgency for keeping the initial resolution was twofold: I wanted to support my daughter in her commitment, and my own health needed serious attention. In fact, looking back, my strong suspicion is that our daughter told me of her resolution in the hope that I would accompany her for my own good as well as hers!

This same dynamic is true of people in their spiritual lives and in the lives of organizations, including the parish. Without a clear sense of what needs to change and why, complacency roots us in the way things have always been. We will consider how we will bring about the needed changes we identify in later chapters, but for now, let us focus on establishing this sense of urgency. What is your "why?"

Establishing Urgency: Among People, in the RCIA Process, in the Parish

People: Spiritual growth requires three things:

- continual attentiveness to the promptings of the Holy Spirit,
- the call of Christ to love and serve (especially the least among us),
- and the grace of God, which touches our minds, hearts, and spirits with life and goodness.

As we accompany seekers and others, our job is to help them:

- develop their attentiveness to the Holy Spirit
- listen to the call of Christ to serve others
- recognize God's love and take it to heart

We guide those we accompany toward the truth that is Christ and that is expressed in Catholic teaching and tradition. We accompany them as they develop life that is rooted in faith.

Here is an astounding fact. Each of us is called to a life of holiness. Maybe that doesn't sound astounding to you. Maybe it sounds a little "churchy." But imagine what it means to live every day as a holy person. The bishops at the Second Vatican Council described it this way:

> The Lord Jesus, divine teacher and model of all perfection, preached holiness of life (of which he is the author and maker)

to each and every one of his disciples without distinction: "You, therefore, must be perfect, as your heavenly Father is perfect" (Mt. 5:48). For he sent the Holy Spirit to all to move them interiorly to love God with their whole heart, with their whole soul, with their whole understanding, and with their whole strength (cf. Mk. 12:30), and to love one another as Christ loved them (cf. Jn. 13:34; 15:12) . . . In order to reach this perfection the faithful should use the strength dealt out to them by Christ's gift, so that, following in his footsteps and conformed to his image, doing the will of God in everything, they may wholeheartedly devote themselves to the glory of God and to the service of their neighbor. Thus the holiness of the People of God will grow in fruitful abundance, as is clearly shown in the history of the Church through the life of so many saints. (Dogmatic Constitution on the Church, 40)

We are called to be perfect just as our heavenly Father is perfect. We often tell ourselves that perfection is impossible; holiness is impossible for everyone but the saints. And yet Jesus preached holiness for every one of us "without distinction." It is not only possible that we live a life of holiness, it is urgent that we do so. We keep the vision of holiness in our hearts and minds and continually discern who we are called to be and how we are called to live, applying Christ's command to love God and neighbor to our daily lives. We consider how we are, or are not, living as God desires, and we discern how we need to change in order to more fully live as Christian people in the world. Whether we are reflecting on our own lives or the lives of the people we accompany, it is imperative to keep alive the call to conversion, change of mind, heart, and life, establishing urgency in order to grow as children of God and members of Christ's body.

Process: How well does the RCIA, as it is currently enacted, serve in your parish? Think for a time about the aspects of the RCIA process in your parish. Talk with RCIA team members. Read and study the *Rite of Christian Initiation of Adults*. Reconnect with previous participants. Examine the ways in which you offer spiritual guidance, accompany seekers in each period of the process, teach the essence of our Catholic Christian faith, enact the liturgical rites, and encourage and support neophytes as they develop patterns of living as fully initiated members of the faith community. What contributes to the effectiveness of your current process? What needs to change?

Keep in mind that, like all aspects of our lives of faith, the ways in which you implement the RCIA will never be finished. Seekers bring varying personal experiences, questions, and spiritual maturity to their participation in the process. Your team members may change. Your pastor may change. The needs of your seekers or your parish may change. In all of these circumstances, it is important to hold on to what is positively contributing to the process as it is currently, while always striving to carry it out as well as possible. What most needs to be changed? Identify one or two aspects, and determine why these things are the most important. What would the positive impact be if the necessary changes are made? Making the change is the way you will fulfill your responsibility as a servant leader. The change in people's lives and the life of the parish is your reason for urgency.

Parish: How is the RCIA a catalyst for conversion within the parish? Are the rites of the RCIA celebrated at Sunday liturgy or, when appropriate, at weekday gatherings? Are catechumens dismissed from the Sunday assembly? How do these public rites influence the lives of parishioners? Are there opportunities for members of the community to meet and become acquainted with seekers and neophytes?

The RCIA serves as witness and call. Participants and the team give witness to the power of a deep and growing relationship with Jesus Christ through their lives in what they say and do. The presence of these people who clearly embrace a life of conversion in Christ inspire and call others to this life and encourage people to open their minds, hearts, and lives to the transforming love of God. In what ways does the RCIA serve as witness and call in your parish?

Questions to Ask Yourself:
Establishing an Urgent Vision

What most stands out in your mind and heart as you think about the people involved in the RCIA (including yourself), the way the RCIA process is carried out, and your parish?

What changes are urgently needed, and why?

Who should you draw into thought and possible action with you?

Step 2

Create Your Vision Team

I have long been inspired by one paragraph of At the Beginning of the New Millennium, St. Pope John Paul II's pastoral letter at the turn of the century:

> To make the Church the home and the school of communion: that is the great challenge facing us in the millennium which is now beginning, if we wish to be faithful to God's plan and respond to the world's deepest yearnings. (43)

This is a powerful statement about who we are called to be as followers of Jesus Christ and the potential we have to make a difference in the lives of others. Discipleship is not a "me and Jesus" endeavor. Ongoing conversion in Christ calls us from being focused on "me" to being part of a "we." "As I have loved you, so you also should love one another," Jesus commands us (John 13:34). As St. John Paul II so aptly notes, it is not only that we are to draw one another deeply to communion with Christ. Our embrace of living discipleship as members of Christ's body, the church, will have lasting impact on the world as we share our gifts, resources, and faith with others. People need to be touched by the love of God and of other people. We learn to live as we are called—with one another. Forming people as disciples is necessarily formation for and through the Christian community.

It can be difficult to speak of community in today's culture, which prizes individuality and self-reliance. The truth is, for most people, living as a member of a community is hard. It is challenging enough to take into consideration the feelings and needs of family and close friends. Thinking of ourselves as a part of yet another community may seem beyond our capacity. For Christians, living in community is not a trivial thing. Membership in the faith community is about much more than signing up or showing up. To truly be part of the Christian community, we must come to trust and rely on one another. We must grow in our attentiveness to others, recognizing that in Christ, each person is essential; all are valued.

A spirituality of communion also means an ability to think of our brothers and sisters in faith within the profound unity of the Mystical Body, and therefore as "those who are a part of me." This makes us able to share their joys and sufferings, to sense their desires and attend to their needs, to offer them deep and genuine friendship. (At the Beginning of the New Millennium, 43)

Of course, this understanding of community is profoundly eucharistic. In Christ, we learn that God's way is the way of self-giving love. Jesus's sacrifice on the cross is redemptive and radical. Christ's model and mandate is to live for others and to recognize Christ in the other. The Eucharist leads us into this radical way of living. We participate in the celebration of the Eucharist alongside one another. We hear the words of Sacred Scripture and the homily with others in the assembly. We offer prayers for the needs of the world and the local community together; and together, we bring our gifts for consecration. Receiving Holy Communion draws us into communion with Christ, and that calls us into community with one another. The deeper our belonging within the community of faith, the fuller our living of faith will be (see Albert Winseman, *Growing an Engaged Church*, 44).

The RCIA: Immersion in Community

We might think of the RCIA as a workshop in such communal living. Team members and participants come together intentionally for the express purpose of growing as Catholic Christian people. Through the rites, dismissal, and extended formation sessions, all who are part of the RCIA reflect on readings from Sacred Scripture, take to heart church teaching, and hold up their lives alongside the gospel. We hear one another's stories and together discern the ways in which we are called to shape our lives as a result of our shared reflections. We appreciate the change of life that discipleship entails, encouraging one another, particularly participants, to embrace Christ and take steps toward faith-filled and faithful living. Participants may find that family and friends struggle with the change of life they are accepting and come to rely on team members and one another for support and encouragement. "Since the Lord in whom they believe is a sign of contradiction, the newly converted often experience divisions and separations, but they also taste the joy that God gives without measure" (RCIA 75.2).

For many, the RCIA process is the first time they experience a true sense of community, and it can take a while to become accustomed to sharing and growing in faith with others in such a deep way. Yet, it is exactly this environment that is needed in order to lead people toward the fullness of faith, hope, and charity. The RCIA must be more than a succession of classes on a wide range of doctrinal topics. If the process is to be transformational, it will be accomplished in the context of the community of believers.

But what does this mean in practice? Here too, our thoughts could run immediately to the action to be undertaken, but that would not be the right impulse to follow. Before making practical plans, we need to promote a spirituality of communion, making it the guiding principle of education wherever individuals and Christians are formed, wherever ministers of the altar, consecrated persons, and pastoral workers are trained, wherever families and communities are being built up. A spirituality of communion indicates above all the heart's contemplation of the mystery of the Trinity dwelling in us, and whose light we must also be able to see shining on the face of the brothers and sisters around us. (At the Beginning of the New Millennium, 43)

Moving from "me" to "we" is a process of formation in a spirituality of communion. Some seekers are challenged and moved by this call to communion. Belonging within a community of faith has dramatic impact on those who are lifelong Catholics and those who have little to no prior religious experience. Indeed, everyone. We are more likely to embrace the call to ongoing conversion in Christ when we are part of a community that is committed to this life of change. What comprises this spirituality of communion? How do we lead one another to a deep encounter and relationship with Christ? As people who are in communion with Christ and one another, we

- "think of our brothers and sisters in faith within the profound unity of the Mystical Body [of Christ], and therefore as 'those who are a part of me' ";

- know that "the Lord has taken the initiative, he has loved us first . . . , and therefore we can move forward, boldly take the initiative, go out to others, seek those who have fallen away, stand at the crossroads and welcome the outcast";

- share one another's joys and sufferings, and sense others' desires and attend to their needs;

- get involved in people's daily lives, as it "bridges distances";

- "see what is positive in others, to welcome it and prize it as a gift from God";

- "know how to 'make room' for our brothers and sisters, bearing 'each other's burdens' ";

- resist "the selfish temptations which constantly beset us and provoke competition, careerism, distrust and jealousy."

(At the Beginning of the New Millennium, 43; Joy of the Gospel, 24)

The RCIA: Home and School of Communion

When you enact the RCIA as a process of formation for discipleship in community, you develop a spirituality of communion. It is the experience of this communion that many previous RCIA team members and participants recall with such fondness. They are often not able to fully articulate their experience, as it transcends typical categories of learning, sharing, growing, and committing oneself to a life of faith. It is all this and more. When considered in this light, the RCIA is a home and school of communion and stands as a beacon for the wider parish community in this regard. Inspired and challenged by the conversion members of the community witness among RCIA participants and team members, they are led to embrace and witness to the power of conversion in Christ in their own lives. "The initiation of catechumens is a gradual process that takes place within the community of the faithful. By joining the catechumens in reflecting on the value of the paschal mystery and by renewing their own conversion, the faithful provide an example that will help the catechumens to obey the Holy Spirit more generously" (RCIA 4).

Leadership from Within

We are establishing a vision of a community of disciples that is always on a journey of conversion in Christ. Moving toward this vision requires leadership. The vision will never be fully realized; leaders must recognize and accept this fact and be ready to steadily guide the community toward the vision for the long term. Remember that we are all leaders. Some have formal positions of leadership, such as the pastor and other clergy, staff members, and members of the parish council and other guiding groups. Others might not currently view themselves as leaders and yet are vital to the development of the faith community as well. As we have already stated, RCIA team members and those who are in any way involved in parish ministries, organizations, and groups are also leaders. This understanding will become crucial in the step toward change that we will explore later in this chapter.

We lead the community from within the community. We might think of this as leadership from the inside out! As leaders, we come from, represent, and influence the faith community. We bear witness to the change in our lives and the lives of others that results from being attentive to the presence of God and responding to the call of Christ. We accept the invitation to serve through the particular roles we fulfill, as an RCIA coordinator or team member or other parish leader. We lead others to embrace this powerful way of life, and we do so from within the community, thereby forming the community as disciples.

Accompanying One Another toward Communion

There is something else we should consider at this stage, and that is our call to accompany one another on the spiritual journey, especially in the RCIA. Spiritual growth is about responding to God's grace. Christian disciples gradually become more attentive to this grace and shape their lives accordingly. As followers of Jesus Christ, we understand that this response will not always be easy, nor will discerning what to do and how to do it always be clear. Having another who accompanies us on this spiritual path is more than something nice to have. It is essential, vital to our acceptance of the call to ongoing conversion, to embracing the change necessary for growth as disciples. Mary Catherine Hilkert, OP, speaks of ministers of the word (which naturally include those who form people through the RCIA) as helping people to name God's grace and to respond to it with their lives (see *Naming Grace*). I believe this is a helpful image for the relationship of spiritual accompaniment we are considering: as people who accompany seekers, we are "namers of grace."

Let us connect this spiritual accompaniment with our previous reflection on the development of a spirituality of communion within the RCIA and the wider parish as a faith community. Surely it would be beneficial to establish accompanying relationships among RCIA team members with seekers, team members with one another, and among parishioners. There could be little doubt that such relationships would result in a deeper sense of communion with Christ and with one another; such communion would certainly result in more powerful expressions of the love of God within the parish and beyond it.

What would change if we took Pope Francis's imperative to stand on the holy ground of the other to heart (Joy of the Gospel, 169)? How might our relationships with one another be affected? What about the RCIA process? How might the process be structured so that team members could more effectively accompany seekers? What could be initiated within the parish so that parishioners might more readily turn to one another as accompanists or companions on the journey of discipleship? Might establishing spiritual companionship change the culture of the parish in such a manner that the parish more closely resembles a home and school of communion?

Who accompanies you on your journey of faith? How does this person influence the way you live and grow as a disciple? Whom do you accompany? What do you perceive is the impact of this relationship?

Spiritual Accompaniment in the RCIA

Picture your RCIA process as it is now. Think of what happens when a new seeker begins to inquire about the faith. Who talks with the seeker? What are the initial topics of conversation? At what point would the inquirer be introduced to team members and other members of the parish? Would he or she be linked to a team member or group? I do not believe there are definitive answers for any of these sorts of questions. However, it seems to me that considering the process of establishing relationships within the RCIA with the goal of spiritual accompaniment would be beneficial for everyone, not only those who are part of the RCIA, but the entire parish. If your process already includes a dimension of spiritual companionship, consider how such relationships might be enhanced or deepened. If your process is currently focused solely or primarily on learning about the faith, think about and move toward a process of faith formation in which seekers are accompanied on their journey to Christ, faith within the Catholic Church, initiation, and a life of discipleship.

Spiritual Accompaniment in the Parish

Think of the many aspects of life within your parish in which people are already drawn to one another as friends, for support, and in ministry to and with one another. Consider all of the small groups within the parish—not only formal small faith communities, but groups such as the choir, altar society, liturgical ministries, social concerns and service groups, religious education families, and so on. How do people already encourage one another in faith within these groups? What would it take to introduce the idea of spiritual accompaniment to members of these groups? What preparation or formation would help people to be ready to accompany others? Does this need to be a formal process within the parish, or could it be accomplished through awareness and the witness of those who have benefited from such relationships in the past?

Change: What and Why

In chapter 1, you began to develop a short list of elements in need of change in your own spiritual life and that of others involved in the RCIA, in your RCIA process, and in your parish. You considered what needed to change and why. Take a moment now to review that list in light of our exploration in this chapter on communion in community. Did your view widen substantially as you consider the vision of a community of disciples on an ongoing journey of conversion in Christ? Did anything come to mind upon which you can build? In what ways do you envision fostering a spirituality of communion within the RCIA and in the parish? Add to or amend your list to reflect your thoughts and discussions as we prepare to consider the second step of the change leadership process.

Leading for Change, Step 2: Create a Vision Team

Have you ever tried to change something in your life or at your parish and simply got stuck? You saw the need to do something. You may have talked to others about this and perhaps thought you had convinced them to get on board with your idea. You might have developed a strategy or plan and perhaps even took initial steps to make the change. Yet, in the end, things remained pretty much as they had been. As you talked with others about it, you realized they never saw the situation exactly as you did. They may have not agreed with your plan, or they simply had not thought about it enough to decide whether or what action was needed. This is a common occurrence and is often the result of attempting a change alone or with others who were either not sufficiently committed to the change or who did not have enough influence to successfully bring it about.

Kotter's second step of change leadership is to create a vision team, what he calls a guiding coalition. No matter how strongly we might feel that change is needed, we will not be able to accomplish what we set out to do if we attempt to do so alone. Effecting change is not up to one person but is dependent upon the direction, guidance, and energy of a group of people who have the authority and ability to lead the change effort within the community. The initial vision team can be relatively small and functions within the existing parish leadership structure, which we will consider in what follows.

Driving Change Together: The Vision Team

We will think about the vision team specifically in relationship to the RCIA and the parish later in this chapter. For now, let us focus on the team's role, composition, and the way it functions in order to bring about change.

What the Vision Team Does

A vision team is a group of people who work within the community to bring about needed change. The group might be an already existing advisory or leadership group, but it is more likely that the team will be formed specifically to lead a change initiative. The vision team develops a common goal and discerns what needs to happen in order to make the goal a reality. The group discerns how change needs to happen and what steps are called for in order to bring about the identified change. They understand the urgency of the change and communicate the urgency to all who will be affected as the change is implemented.

Let me share one experience of change in the way the RCIA was carried out in my parish. When I became the RCIA coordinator, the parish had an academic year program that began in mid-September and ended the week after the Easter Vigil. It did not matter what the person's spiritual growth, prior understanding of Catholic teaching, or personal situation was. Unless there was a previous marriage that impeded initiation, everyone who began the process in September was initiated at the Easter Vigil. If someone inquired about Catholicism in January, he or she was told that the program began the following September. You get the picture.

My pastor and I had talked at length about the need to move to a year-round RCIA process. I knew I had his direction and support to proceed. I also realized that the people who had been part of the RCIA in the past and the parish community itself would need help in understanding the reasons for the change that was to come. I was fortunate that the parish had a faith formation advisory commission with whom I consulted, as well as new RCIA team members who immediately agreed with the planned direction.

I would now call these people a guiding coalition. They represented many constituents within the process and the parish; they reported the plan and progress toward it to the pastoral council; they advised me as we made our way through the first tentative year; and they evaluated our progress in succeeding years, until it was clear that year-round RCIA had become normative.

Without the team, our move from an academic program to a year-round process would likely have been met with resistance and could easily have gotten stuck. Those who did not see the urgency in making the change could have stalled progress; a handful of people could have become obstacles as the change was initiated; the community could have been confused; new seekers could have been turned away, delayed, or turned off. As a result of the service of the vision team, however, the change took place with only a few unanticipated wrinkles. The community grew spiritually as they experienced the rites on a more regular basis and began to grasp their responsibility to witness to their faith and invite others to inquire. Participants were not hurried through the process, which became focused on comprehensive faith formation rather than a brief succession of doctrinal classes. The shifts were simultaneously theological, spiritual, and practical for the RCIA team, participants, and the parish.

Who the Vision Team Is

Ideally, the vision team is comprised of people with varied talents who can communicate the need for change, create a plan to bring the change about, and implement it often by collaborating with others. The team should have at least some authority, either explicit (as when the pastor or his designated staff person is part of the coalition) or implicit (as when the RCIA coordinator and team discern how the process will be structured or who will lead specific portions of the process). The guiding coalition should include people who share a common goal, understand the reasons for the anticipated change, grasp its urgency, and are able to articulate what is being planned and why in a compelling manner to all who will be affected. Therefore, it is helpful for the team to include members that are connected to the elements of parish life that will be involved in the change.

In a parish, it is important for the pastor to be on board with the anticipated change and either directly participate in the plans or make his support known to the guiding group as well as the pastoral council and wider parish community. Other coalition members may include a staff member, pastoral council or committee member, and parishioners who represent the various constituencies that comprise the aspect(s) of parish life that could be impacted by the change.

John Kotter points to three essential elements to build a coalition that can make change happen (68):

Find the right people

- The coalition needs to have the authority to make the change happen, broad expertise, and high credibility. In parish life, if the pastor is not part of the coalition, who are his delegates? What roles within the parish are represented? Does this group have the authority to lead for change? How are they perceived by other parishioners, staff, and the pastor and other clergy?

- Find people with leadership and management skills, especially leadership.

Create trust

- Provide carefully planned exercises to build a strong team.

- Include lots of talk and joint activities.

Develop a common goal

- Make it sensible to the head.

- Appeal to the heart.

In the example of adopting a year-round RCIA process, the vision team included two members of the RCIA team and three members of the faith formation commission. Members of the group met with the worship commission and the music director, since the change would impact when the rites would be celebrated and would necessitate more frequent Sunday dismissals. The group also provided details to the pastoral council and the parish staff. Coalition members wrote articles that they published in the parish bulletin and newsletter. The pastor referred to the change in his homily occasionally, encouraging parishioners to witness to their faith and be aware of family and friends who might be seeking faith, initiation or completion of initiation, at any time of the year. Coalition members were attentive to potential roadblocks and adjusted the plan as needed throughout the process.

Two Caveats

Kotter points to two primary pitfalls of which we should be particularly aware at the stage of building a guiding coalition. The first is to acknowledge potential opposition to the change, especially among members of the guiding group. If the anticipated change is emotionally charged (which many elements of parish life are), it is likely that you will experience some opposition. It is important to acknowledge this and to plan to address such response if or when it emerges. It is fine to include someone in the coalition who is less than enthusiastic about the change. In fact, it could be beneficial if that person's participation would ensure the eventual acceptance among a contingent of parishioners or parish groups. That person should be carefully selected, and his or her involvement must be managed in order to provide opportunities for him or her to contribute without negatively impacting the process.

Second, we must carefully manage team members who are highly ego- or control-driven. While we might want to think that such issues never occur in parish ministry, anyone who has been involved in parish life long enough realizes that such issues do, indeed, exist from time to time. Being watchful of the potential for members who agree to be part of the coalition in order to feed their sense of self-worth or who want to control aspects of the life of the parish is crucial, especially in the early stages of the process of change.

How the Vision Team Functions

The way in which the vision team functions will depend upon the change that has been identified and the circumstances that surround the change. As the example above illustrates, the coalition grasps the need for change, articulates the urgency to others, creates a plan to enact the change, and implements the plan. We will continue to explore the function of the coalition in what follows. For now, consider who would be appropriate members of your vision team. Like your short list of needed changes, your potential vision team will take shape as you continue to study and discuss the process of change leadership.

A Spiritual "Vision Team"

The need for a vision team may seem perfectly sensible when considering change in the RCIA process or the parish. It may not immediately be apparent how this applies to the spiritual life of people, however, until we consider this in the context of our previous exploration of spiritual accompaniment in community. When we accompany others or are accompanied ourselves, we help one another to hear and respond to the voice of God. We hold the vision of lifelong conversion before us and those we accompany. Discernment is a communal endeavor. It is difficult to see ourselves clearly, to recognize and turn away from temptation, and to determine the best way forward on our own. Having another who listens and helps us to perceive God's grace and call is essential if we are to embrace ongoing conversion. "Only through such respectful and compassionate listening can we enter on the paths of true growth and awaken a yearning for the Christian ideal: the desire to respond fully to God's love and bring to fruition what he has sown in our lives" (Joy of the Gospel, 171).

In addition to the willingness to listen, the spiritual accompaniment relationship relies on trust, confidentiality, a commitment to hear observations that may be difficult, and a willingness to consider possibilities that seem spiritually or practically challenging. Having a personal guiding coalition may happen in the context of spiritual direction, mentorship, or a less formal mutual relationship of spiritual companionship.

Questions to Ask Yourself: Vision Teams

A Vision Team for the RCIA

Who is responsible for shaping the RCIA and implementing it in your parish? If you are the coordinator, do you have team members or others whom you consult? If you are a team member, do you have regular opportunities to share ideas with the coordinator? How would the RCIA coordinator and team raise issues or share ideas related to the RCIA or the parish with the pastor, pastoral council, or faith formation committee? These may sound like abstract questions, but they are central to the process of effecting change.

A Vision Team for the Parish

How are decisions currently made in your parish? Is there an existing structure of leadership in which elements of parish life are examined and adjustments are made when necessary? How are new ideas considered?

If, in your reading of this book and discussing it with others, you identify areas of change that are needed in the way the RCIA is shaped and implemented in your parish or in the ways the RCIA might influence the life and function of the parish, consider the composition of a guiding coalition in order to create the greatest opportunity to lead for change.

Questions for Discussion

What is your experience? How do members of the RCIA team and RCIA participants experience a spirituality of communion with Christ and with one another in your parish?

Do you have a group that functions as a guiding coalition? Is this a formal group or informal one? What is its role at present? What would enhance the ways in which this group contributes in the future?

Step 3

Make Your Vision a Reality

In the previous two chapters, we have established a vision and we have talked about the team you need for the vision. It is a vision of the parish as a community of disciples that is on an ongoing journey of conversion in Christ.

We also outlined some steps that will help us lead for and manage the change necessary to enact this vision in the RCIA and in the parish.

Thus far, we have spoken in ideal terms, looking at the big picture. Now, it is time to get more practical. We need to be clear about what we hope for and to identify initial steps to help us bring the vision to life.

Diving Deeply into the Paschal Mystery

Susan came to the RCIA just after Christmas. She had been invited to join a friend at Christmas Mass and was touched by the experience. Somehow, she knew there was something there for her. At first, it was difficult to put it into words, but after a few months' participation in the RCIA process, she began to grasp what it was that compelled her to come. In talking with one of the team members, she said, "I just never thought that God could love me so much. I always thought God was distant and judgmental; but what I heard and felt at Christmas is that God wants to be close to me. Me! Susan! And to everyone!"

Susan's experience would have been different had her first Mass been at Easter, or a Sunday in Ordinary Time. The Holy Spirit might have spoken to her heart differently. Of course, each Sunday liturgy is a celebration of the fullness of Christ's love. Yet, through the liturgical feasts and seasons, we are invited to reflect on particular aspects of the paschal mystery and to connect these with our lives in real and transformative ways. In celebrating and reflecting on the mystery of God's love for us in Christ through the Sundays and seasons of the liturgical year, we are changed. This is why it is so important that the RCIA be carried out as a year-long process. And this is why the RCIA says:

> A suitable catechesis is provided by priests or deacons, or by catechists and others of the faithful, planned to be gradual and complete in its coverage, accommodated to the liturgical year, and solidly supported by celebrations of the word. This cate-chesis leads the catechumens not only to an appropriate acquain-tance with dogmas and precepts but also to a profound sense of the mystery of salvation in which they desire to participate. (RCIA 75.1)

This is not to say that people will experience moments of trial only during Lent or of new life during Easter. However, we who have journeyed through many cycles of the liturgical year know how the rhythm of seasons invites us to ponder aspects of the paschal mystery in particular ways. Especially as we consider the manner in which we accompany people through the RCIA, it is important for us to be constantly attentive to signs of interior spiritual growth, struggle, or yearning of participants. Connecting these movements to Christ's life, death, and resurrection brings faith to life for those in the RCIA and all in the parish. Participants, team members, and parishioners are sure to experience obstacles and spiritual darkness, just as surely as they will experience God's presence, encouragement, and new life through faith. We must be prepared to walk with people in every stage of their formation, particularly in their times of difficulty or struggle. Doing so is a sign of Christ's undying love.

Let us take this a step further. We do not simply connect people's experience in life and faith to the life of Christ. We also must help people enter into the mystery of Christ's life, death, and resurrection. Without this essential aspect of spiritual accompaniment, experiences of suffering, trial, questioning, and death, as well as those of life, joy, and peace are empty of the true depth of Christ's saving love.

Taking the Call of Christ to Heart

We celebrated the Rite of Acceptance at Sunday Mass in the late autumn of that first year. After Mass, many people paused to greet the catechumens. People told me the rite had made them think about their own willingness to take up their cross and follow Christ. The following Monday, I received a number of phone calls from parishioners. Some wondered why it was necessary to celebrate the rite at Mass. They saw it as a disruption of "their" prayer time. To be honest, I was not fully prepared for this reaction and later discussed their response with the team. One phone call stood out, however, because the caller put in words what many had said on Sunday after the celebration. The woman called, she said, simply to tell me that she was moved by the signing of the senses (RCIA 55–56) and was "jealous" of the catechumens. "Not only are they taking the call to faith to heart, it is obvious that you and the others are helping them do so. I wish I had that sort of help to grow in faith." It was at that moment that I saw the interrelationship between the RCIA and the parish. Each leads the other to deeper commitment to Christ; each spurs the other on to living discipleship.

Seeking Clarity

Taking to heart the centrality of the liturgy and the role of the liturgical cycle of Sundays and seasons compelled us to move toward the vision of a year-round RCIA process at my parish. Our team often talked about what it was going to take to establish this practice for the long haul. There are many "moving parts" involved, such as

- incorporating seekers as they arrived,

- inviting and forming team members who would be on hand to support newcomers throughout the year,

- adjusting the catechetical sessions to be directed by the Sunday readings,

- discerning the readiness of participants as they moved toward various stages of the rite.

We also understood that moving to a year-round process involved more than the way the process was organized. The parish community needed to be formed. We took to heart the instruction in the Introduction to the RCIA.

> The initiation of catechumens is a gradual process that takes place within the community of the faithful. By joining the catechumens in reflecting on the value of the paschal mystery and by renewing their own conversion, the faithful provide an example that will help the catechumens to obey the Holy Spirit more generously. (RCIA 4)

Yet, even as we made our way through the early months of the transition to the year-round process, we still could not precisely describe why the change was important, nor could we clearly articulate what we hoped would result from the change. We needed clarity in our vision of the process and its impact on people.

For it is the liturgy through which, especially in the divine sacrifice of the Eucharist, "the work of our redemption is accomplished," and it is through the liturgy, especially, that the faithful are enabled to express in their lives and manifest to others the mystery of Christ and the real nature of the true Church. . . . The liturgy daily builds up those who are in the Church, making of them a holy temple of the Lord, a dwelling-place for God in the Spirit, to the mature measure of the fullness of Christ. (Constitution on the Sacred Liturgy, 2)

In 1999, the US bishops published their pastoral plan for adult faith formation, *Our Hearts Were Burning Within Us: A Pastoral Plan for Adult Faith Formation in the United States*. In its introduction, two brief paragraphs succinctly described what we were trying to do at the parish:

> We seek to form *parishes* that are vitally alive in faith. These communities will provide a parish climate and an array of activities and resources designed to help adults more fully understand and live the faith.

> We seek to form *adults* who actively cultivate a lively baptismal and eucharistic spirituality with a powerful sense of mission and apostolate. Nourished by word, sacrament, and communal life, they will witness and share the Gospel in their homes, neighborhoods, places of work, and centers of culture. (17)

These two paragraphs captured our vision. With this succinct statement of purpose, the guiding coalition could see how the "moving parts" contributed to the vision. The faith formation commission understood how the RCIA is the "source of inspiration for all catechesis" (*National Directory for Catechesis*, 35D). No longer was our vision vague or pie-in-the-sky. Not only did we have more clarity about why we were making changes to the ways in which the RCIA was carried out, the guiding coalition and RCIA team could better discern the next steps to be taken and to implement those strategies more effectively.

Getting Clear

Now we are getting clear! "The rite of initiation is suited to a spiritual journey of adults that varies according to the many forms of God's grace, the free cooperation of the individuals, the action of the Church, and the circumstances of time and place" (RCIA 5). Our role as leaders in the RCIA and the wider parish community is to provide for *spiritual growth*.

We had to provide for spiritual growth among participants, team members, and parishioners, to provide the means for people to name and respond to the grace of God in their lives. When, and only when, the RCIA is enacted within a community of adults who are actively and intentionally growing in faith, parish culture develops in which discipleship is normative. The development of this culture is circular:

- Catechumenate formation

- leads to wider parish community formation,

- and back again to catechumenate formation.

When we provide for the spiritual growth of both seekers and parishioners, we are fulfilling the mission of the church to evangelize—to draw people to Jesus Christ and to lead them to live and grow as Christian disciples. Remember what we said in Chapter 1 about fewer people participating in Mass, the declining numbers of people becoming Catholic, and the numbers of young people leaving the faith? One of the most dismaying realities we face as people who are called to evangelize is that two-thirds of those who were raised Catholic and become unaffiliated report that one of their key reasons for doing so is that they did not feel their spiritual needs were being met within Catholicism ("Faith in Flux"). The Gallup Organization's research on parish engagement also points to meeting people's spiritual needs as one of the foundational factors in leading people to spiritual commitment (Winseman, *Growing an Engaged Church*, 81). More recently, qualitative studies done by the Fuller Youth Institute point to taking Jesus's message seriously as one of six core commitments necessary in order to evangelize teens and young adults (Kara Powell, Jake Mulder, and Brad Griffin, *Growing Young*). In other words, ensuring the possibility of spiritual growth among our people is especially crucial in our time.

Forming Individuals in Community

An even cursory study of the RCIA presents leaders with a sense of the deep spiritual journey through which we lead participants. While the journey takes place within the community, there is an individual, personal dimension to the process. Seekers should not be funneled into the stages of the rite lockstep, no more than parishioners would be expected to all be at the same stage of spiritual development at the same time. This awareness is, in reality, the joy and challenge of the RCIA for the coordinator and team, as well as for the wider community, as people experience the various public rites and become acquainted with participants.

This, I believe, brings us back to the value of spiritual accompaniment as an element of the vision we are building for the RCIA and the parish. It will be of great benefit for team members, sponsors, godparents, clergy, and the RCIA coordinator to acquire the ministerial stance of one who accompanies others on the journey of faith. Participants and team members share the value of such relationships with other parishioners; the parishioners grow in their accompaniment of one another, continuing the cycle of evangelization and more deeply forming individuals within the community of faith.

Planning to Carry Out the Vision

By now, it is likely becoming clear that we need a plan to ensure that the RCIA will have the impact that is possible for participants, team members, and the parish. Say the word "plan" at a parish meeting, and watch the reactions. A few people might nod or express interest, but it is likely that more than a few will wince, avert their eyes, and hope that someone, anyone, will change the subject. Why are so many parish leaders averse to planning? Some seem to think that planning is contradictory to being pastoral. Somehow, in this view, having a plan prevents us from timely and appropriate pastoral response.

More people, however, have experienced the pain of long, arduous meetings over the span of many months or more, creating a plan that was never implemented. It may have lacked specificity, realistic expectations, or the resources (people or financial) necessary to carry it out. I have heard this from parish people for years: "We met, and talked, and brainstormed, and talked some more, and ended up with a binder full of notes, and yet we're still right where we were before we did all of that." Yet, as the familiar maxim attributed to Benjamin Franklin reminds us, "If we fail to plan, we plan to fail."

If the word "plan" makes you wince, fear not. I promise the sort of planning I'm talking about will be pastoral and it will be worth every moment of your time! Also be assured that the planning we will discuss will be focused on the RCIA and the spiritual growth of the people of the parish. While much of what we explore here can be applied to the process of developing a pastoral plan for the parish as a whole, we will limit our considerations here in keeping with the focus of this book and its process.

Let us briefly address those two reactions I described above. There is no doubt that our parishes must respond pastorally to the needs of our individuals and the parish. What leaders sometimes miss is that this pastoral response is actually more possible when a pastoral plan is in place—people, ministries, and resources will have been allocated, and processes for pastoral response will have been developed in advance. Second, planning need not be arduous, nor should it be an exercise in futility. In fact, as is so often the case, the simpler, the better where planning is concerned.

Change: What and Why

Kotter points to the importance of having a clear, succinct vision of what needs to change and what the needed change would look like when it is accomplished. He outlines seven steps for creating an effective vision, while insisting that simplicity is essential (84). Here are his steps:

Creating an Effective Vision

- **First draft**: The process often starts with an initial statement from a single individual, reflecting both his or her dreams and the real needs of the organization.

- **Role of the guiding coalition**: The first draft is always modeled over time by the guiding coalition or even a larger group of people.

- **Importance of teamwork**: The group process never works well with a minimum of effective teamwork.

- **Role of the head and the heart**: Both analytical thinking and a lot of dreaming are essential throughout the activity.

- **Messiness of the process**: Vision creation is usually a process of two steps forward and one back, movement to the left and then to the right.

- **Time frame**: Vision is never created in a single meeting. The activity needs time.

- **End product**: The process results in a direction for the future that is desirable, feasible, focused, flexible, and is conveyable in five minutes or less.

Gain Clarity of Vision

Develop your first draft: pause for a few moments and write a statement that captures your vision for the RCIA in your community. Don't worry about using churchy language. In fact, avoid churchy language. In just a few sentences, describe how the RCIA would be carried out and what the impact of it would be in your vision. Be as succinct as possible while still conveying the essence of where you hope to be a year or two from now. Be intelligent as you think this through. You may not know all of the details of what it will take to get to this vision. That is just fine at this point. Be as specific as possible while not getting into too much detail. The details will come later.

Look back at your notes from the previous two chapters. What aspects of what you have read and discussed with others should be included in your vision statement? What would change if the vision came to be?

If you are reading and reacting to this book on your own, now is a good time to share your reflections with others. Consider forming a guiding coalition if you have not already done so. Keep in mind that the coalition often includes people who are involved in the RCIA or in parish leadership (formally as a pastor, deacon, or staff person or informally as a parishioner leader). The coalition also often includes a few people who are not already involved as leaders but who are passionate about the changes you are considering. The passion and commitment of the coalition is essential to the process of leading for change.

Getting Clear Takes Time

As Kotter notes in his steps for the development of the vision above, the process of gaining a clear, succinct, and actionable vision takes time. I would suggest that you not continue to the next chapter until you have developed a clear vision statement. Time spent here will make everything that follows not only easier but more possible and more effective. Use the table at the end of this chapter to develop your vision statement, and record it in the column labeled Dream. I have provided three sections in the table corresponding to the three aspects of people, process, and parish that we are using to organize our thoughts and plans. You might draw all three together into one vision statement or keep them separate in order to focus your attention as you develop strategies in what follows.

Be Honest about What Is Currently in Place

With your vision firmly in mind, it is time to describe how the RCIA is carried out currently. Be attentive to what is already in place and how it positively contributes to the lives of the participants, process, or parish. Keep notes about things that need attention or change, but do not dwell on this for now. That will come in the next step. For now, capture the current state of the RCIA as clearly as possible.

What aspects of the way in which the RCIA is currently enacted contribute to the vision for the future you have described above? What people, resources, and processes are already in place?

Use the table at the end of the chapter to record the current status in relationship to people, the RCIA process, and the parish in the column labeled Discover. Focus on what is already contributing positively at this point. Make notes about potential aspects of change that you will discern in the next step.

Taking Intentional Steps toward the (Now Clearer) Vision

I often describe the process of planning for change as knowing where we are and where we want to be, and then discerning what steps will help us get there. Imagine yourself standing on a line looking at a line a few feet ahead of where you are standing. In order to get from where you are to where you want to be (that line just ahead of you), you have to take a step. That is what we will do in order to plan for change. We will take a realistic look at what is currently in place, especially what is working, and get clear about the vision of where we want to go. Then, it is a simple process of determining our immediate next steps.

Leading for Change, Step 3:
Develop Initial Strategies

You have articulated your vision for the future, and you have outlined what is currently in place that contributes to that vision. Now it is time to discern your immediate next steps. What needs to change in order to move one step (or two steps) closer to your vision? Be specific at this point about what needs to happen, but do not actually begin to lay out your plan. Record your initial thoughts in the Discern column in the table below. Keep in mind that the strategies and plans you develop here will be flexible and may change over time. One of the great assets of this process is that you may easily adapt as you proceed, which we will explore in greater detail in chapters 4 through 8.

Use the "Appreciative Inquiry" table below to develop a simple plan for initiating change.

	Discover Identify current experience or practice. What is "working?"	**Dream** What is your vision? What are your hopes, dreams, and prayers?	**Discern** What should be? What changes are necessary?	**Do** What will be? What will you do to take a step closer to your vision?
People: Reflect on your personal spiritual life and that of the RCIA team and participants. How are you, individually and as a community, growing in holiness?				
Process: Consider your current RCIA practices. In what ways are participants provided spiritual accompaniment? How are participants led to an encounter with God's love? How are they drawn to the truth of Christ and to the essentials of Catholic teaching?				
Parish: What is your experience of life in your parish at present? How does your parish fulfill its mission? In what ways does the RCIA witness and call toward living discipleship in your parish?				

Step 4

Share Your Vision

It never fails to strike me—that moment in which someone shares his or her story of conversion. Faith that was once dormant becomes a living force in a person's life, or a person's new relationship with Jesus simply must be shared with others. There is a power in hearing how others are touched by the Holy Spirit; are drawn to the heart of God; grow to call Jesus brother, Savior, and friend; realize in the church a home, mother, bearer of truth, and community; and recognize Christ in the other, prompting them to reach out with God's love and mercy.

The impulse to share such experiences is at the heart of what it means to evangelize and is one of the reasons why, as Catholics, we understand evangelization as something that happens over and over to us and with us and through us.

> All of us are called to offer others an explicit witness to the saving love of the Lord, who despite our imperfections offers us his closeness, his word and his strength, and gives meaning to our lives. In your heart you know that it is not the same to live without him; what you have come to realize, what has helped

you to live and given you hope, is what you also need to communicate to others. (Joy of the Gospel, 121)

This is not a once-in-a-lifetime happening because God continues to work with us throughout our lives. And hearing how God is working with one of us, or a group among us, inspires all of us.

My dear young friends, I want to invite you to "dare to love." Do not desire anything less for your life than a love that is strong and beautiful and that is capable of making the whole of your existence a joyful undertaking of giving yourselves as a gift to God and your brothers and sisters, in imitation of the One who vanquished hatred and death forever through love. Love is the only force capable of changing the heart of the human person and of all humanity, by making fruitful the relations between men and women, between rich and poor, between cultures and civilizations. (Pope Benedict XVI, World Youth Day, 2007)

The Power of Conversion and the RCIA

By participating in the RCIA process, the seekers and the team are especially graced to grow in faith together. The RCIA process also stands as witness to the wider parish community. Through liturgical rites, regular dismissal from the Sunday assembly, and opportunities for participants to witness to the conversion that is taking place in their lives, parishioners are drawn to consider the impact of faith in their own lives. As parishioners experience rites such as the Rite of Acceptance into the Order of Catechumens and the scrutinies, they are invited to examine what it means to be initiated into the life of Christ, their own commitment as disciples, and their need for conversion. Participants' presence in the Liturgy of the Word reminds parishioners that Christ is present in the word proclaimed and that reflecting on the Sunday readings is not a task but a privilege. Catechumens' dismissal from the Sunday assembly leads parishioners to consider their appreciation of the Eucharist and call to live as eucharistic people. When parishioners see the impact of the RCIA, we have an opportunity to help them connect this experience with the desire God has planted within each of us to be closer to God and to the people around us.

How has the story of conversion of a friend or experience of an RCIA participant had an impact on your own experience of God and relationship with Jesus?

How are stories of growing faith and conversion shared within your parish?

Faith Formation of Adults Is Normative?

In many ways, we can look at what happens within the initiation process and see it as the model for everyone. Within the RCIA community, people enter into relationships of trust, grapple with the demands of discipleship, and grow in their relationship with Christ and the church. Any who have spent time in the catechumenate process—as team members or participants—are likely to find resonance with the early community of believers as described in the Acts of the Apostles:

> They devoted themselves to the teaching of the apostles and to the communal life, to the breaking of the bread and to the prayers. Awe came upon everyone, and many wonders and signs were done through the apostles. All who believed were together and had all things in common; they would sell their property and possessions and divide them among all according to each one's need. Every day they devoted themselves to meeting together in the temple area and to breaking bread in their homes. They ate their meals with exultation and sincerity of heart, praising God and enjoying favor with all the people. And

every day the Lord added to their number those who were being
saved. (Acts 2:42-47)

Like the community that is described in Acts, participants in the
RCIA are formed in faith. Their lives are shaped through an ongoing encounter with Christ that is experienced with others who
are being formed in similar ways. The very life of the community is
formative—people spend time with each other, worship and learn
side by side, and are drawn beyond themselves to care for others.
This life is compelling. It leads people to take on Christ's very life.

Those who are involved in the RCIA often wish that all in the parish could experience it or something very much like it. It isn't only
those who are part of the RCIA process who have this desire. Most
RCIA coordinators hear at least occasionally that parishioners wish
there could be something akin to "RCIA for Catholics." In other
words, other adults in the community see the value of the process
and want it for themselves. They may not know what happens in
the RCIA but are inspired by the conversion they see in participants
and recognize something that is missing in their own lives.

The catechetical documents speak of adult faith formation as
being normative, "the principal form of catechesis, because it is
addressed to persons who have the greatest responsibilities and
the capacity to live the Christian message in its fully developed
form" (On Catechesis in Our Time, 43). "Because of its importance
and because all other forms of catechesis are oriented in some way
to it, the catechesis of adults must have high priority at all levels
of the Church" (*National Directory for Catechesis*, 48A). (Remember,
too, the quote from *Our Hearts Were Burning Within Us*, which we
read in chapter 3, that spoke about parishes providing a climate
that would help adults more fully understand and live the faith.)
And yet, adult faith formation is hit-and-miss in most parishes.
Diving into all of the dynamics of adult faith formation and why
it is often sparse in parishes is beyond the scope of this book. Yet,
there is an interrelationship that must be acknowledged in order
to more fully grasp the potential influence of the RCIA in the life
of the parish.

The Influence of the RCIA as Faith Formation in Community

The more fully the RCIA is enacted as a process of faith formation within a loving community, the more likely it is that other adults in the parish will desire such formation and grow as disciples who live and share their faith:

- Parishioners see in participants examples of people who are falling in love with Christ and whose lives are being shaped by faith.

- RCIA participants model openness to encountering Christ and to a life of conversion. Growth in faith is understood to be gradual and lifelong.

- Throughout the entire year, RCIA participants and parishioners become more responsive to the working of the Holy Spirit. Knowing that the process is available throughout the year, parishioners encourage family and friends to enter into the RCIA process when they are ready.

- The rhythm of the liturgical year, with its immersion in the paschal mystery, becomes the rhythm of life within the parish and in the lives of the people.

- Parishioners grow in the ways they value the community of faith and their desire to become more fully a part of it.

- As they experience the enthusiasm and fervor of participants, parishioners are more likely to hear the call to discipleship and ongoing conversion.

- As a result, the parish and its people become more likely to share their faith with others, to evangelize (*General Directory for Catechesis*, 91; *National Directory for Catechesis*, 35D, 48A).

Relationships Matter

It is not only that the RCIA process and the rest of parish life are interrelated. Relationships are key to all that we have described above. As RCIA participants and team members interact with parishioners, all are spurred to living and growing in faith. We cannot overlook the importance of relationships. And in fact, everything we know about religiosity in our time points to the importance of the community in engaging people in a relationship with Christ.

Let me say that a bit more clearly: being rooted in relationships with one another as members of Christ's body leads us to a deeper relationship with Christ. We experience Christ's presence with one another. This is one of the reasons why hearing one another's conversion stories is so crucial. When we see the power of God working in others, we become more convinced that God will work with us as well.

Let us take this a step further. As we consider the aspects of the way in which the RCIA is enacted within the parish, it is vital that we see the process within the context of the wider faith community. The RCIA team and participants often experience an intimate sense of community with one another. As important as this is, it is imperative that the process does not become insular and separate from the parish. Rather, the RCIA is to be seen as a community within the community, a deep expression of what it means to be and to become members of Christ's body, the church.

Relationships matter. This is no surprise. In fact, it is consistent with our deep conviction that faith is not only a "me and Jesus thing" but is experienced, developed, and informed through participation in the Christian community. Even with this recognition, however, many, perhaps most, parishes fail to intentionally build a strong sense of community. Instead, we tend to think of relationships as a by-product of our participation in the Sunday Mass, service and outreach, and occasional social gatherings. As we continue to explore aspects of the RCIA and parish life that are in need of development and change, it is good for us to keep this in mind. While we may think structurally about the way the RCIA is shaped and carried out and the influence of the RCIA on the parish, it is important for us to be attentive to any and all opportunities to build relationships among team members, participants, and parishioners.

Conversion in Community

As we noted earlier, by envisioning the RCIA and parish life itself as processes of conversion in community, we are exploring a significant change within the RCIA and the parish. The two—the RCIA and the parish—are interrelated. It is necessary for us to keep this in mind as we lead for and manage change, since what happens in one influences what takes place in the other. When the RCIA is carried out in a year-round process, with communal celebrations of the liturgical rites, Sunday dismissals, and within the context of the parish community, we are safe to expect that the parish will be influenced toward more vibrant, compelling, living faith.

As the parish grows more deeply as a community of disciples, leadership and involvement in the parish shifts to wider participation among parishioners. This is especially true when parish life is shaped to facilitate such involvement. Again, this is beyond the scope of this book, but I would encourage you to explore the experience of parishes that are fostering stewardship as a way of life if your parish is not already doing so. We want to increase parishioner engagement and to intentionally provide the means for people to express and act on their growing faith within the life of the parish and beyond it. While the designated leaders are still responsible for all that happens within the parish, the direction and sustenance of the parish is shared among parishioners to a greater extent when they are actively engaged and invited to contribute meaningfully. Eventually, most elements of parish life can be coordinated by teams of parishioners under the guidance of the pastor or a staff member. Not only does this make ministry more engaging and manageable, it also ensures that parish life is not immediately or adversely affected by change in staff or pastor.

Change: What and Why

We have previously laid the foundations necessary to foster change in the RCIA and the parish that will make this substantial shift in culture possible:

- **The vision is firmly planted in our hearts and minds**. The RCIA is a process of formation for discipleship leading participants and team members to fully embrace a lifetime of conversion in Christ. The parish community is inspired by the witness of those involved in the RCIA, and the entire parish is drawn more deeply to Christ as a result.

- **A team of people is ready to guide the process**. The guiding coalition holds the vision in front of itself working within the parish to bring about needed change. The coalition leads the RCIA and as much as possible the parish to be formed as the home and school of communion through which people accompany one another on the journey of faith.

- **An initial plan has been developed**. The coalition gains clarity of vision, discerns what change is needed, and develops initial strategies to bring the vision to life.

Pause for a moment to consider what is outlined above. As straightforward as the process may seem, it will take only a few moments to realize that what we have outlined above is only part of what will be necessary in order to truly change the culture of the parish, creating a transformative RCIA process within a community of disciples. Anyone who has been involved in the parish long enough knows that having a plan, even as succinct as the one we outlined in the previous chapter, is only part of the equation.

Consider this:

- A plan is only beneficial if it is implemented. This seems self-evident, and yet many who have been involved in parish planning, even within a single ministry, know that often after weeks or months of discussions and plan development, what is finally developed is printed, placed in binders, and occasionally referenced in meetings with little or no action or implementation.

- Carrying out the plan must be more than walking through steps and checking things off a list. Some plans are implemented at least to a certain degree. But even then, the plan often fails to result in the lasting transformation that is hoped for.

- Those who develop the plan bear responsibility for bringing others into the hoped-for change. Often, plan developers grasp the reasons for it and what is necessary to carry it out, but this understanding remains with the small group involved in the planning process.

This is not only a parish thing, in fact. It is an organizational reality. Too often, leaders or those who are charged with guiding an element of the life of an organization create a plan and it remains only that, a plan. Or, it is minimally implemented. Or, the plan remains in the hands of its developers, never reaching the broader organization. And let us be honest here and note that sometimes the plan is not carried out because it would be too disruptive to do so. People would have to change their behavior; common practices might be examined, found in need of change, and adjusted; the status quo would be challenged. At an organizational level, it is easy to see that a plan that is only minimally implemented will have minimal benefit. But we are not talking about just any organization, nor should our plan have only practical implications. What we do or fail to do in the RCIA and the parish has spiritual consequences. Conversion is meant to be disruptive. As disciples, we are constantly called to *metanoia*, to a change of mind and heart, so that we turn away from all that is not of God and turn toward Christ's radical way of life.

If we truly want those who participate in the RCIA and the parish to be communities of disciples who are journeying together in Christ, hearts and minds must be changed. And not only the hearts and minds of those who are designated as leaders. The vision team cannot do this alone, even in partnership with the pastor, staff, and pastoral council. To truly bring about change, many more people will be needed, bringing their talents, gifts, time, energy, insights, and passion to bear. Not only are others needed organizationally. People must take the vision to heart and live it at the parish certainly, but more importantly in their daily lives.

It is time to share the message—of God's love for us in Jesus Christ; the grace of being formed in faith so that it shapes the way we live our lives; the role of the RCIA in forming seekers and urging team members toward deeper commitment as disciples; and the impact of the RCIA on the parish as a community of disciples who journey in faith together.

Tell the Story

Let me return to the example of my first year as the RCIA coordinator at the parish as we consider this together. I have already mentioned that the guiding coalition kept the pastoral council abreast of the developments in the process and worked with the liturgy director and worship commission. The pastor occasionally spoke about the RCIA in the context of his homily, and announcements were made throughout the year to invite seekers to inquire when they were ready. This is not the only way parishioners learned about the shifts that were happening within the process, however. In fact, were it only through occasional announcements at Mass, the vast majority of parishioners would likely not have understood the impact of the process on the lives of participants and team members, nor would they have grasped the implications for their own lives of faith.

We found that the real shifts in awareness happened as we regularly dismissed catechumens from the Sunday assembly and celebrated the Rite of Acceptance into the Order of Catechumens as inquirers were ready. The celebration of the scrutinies, the Sending of the Catechumens for Election, and the Rite of Calling the Candidates to Continuing Conversion the first year were pivotal. But it was only after the Easter Vigil, as we invited the neophytes to speak at the end of Mass, sharing their stories of conversion and faith, and meet with parishioners socially after Mass, that parishioners "got it." It was as though they were suddenly being brought into a new way of thinking, not only about those who were being formed through the RCIA, but about themselves as followers of Jesus Christ. Parishioners spoke of how moving it was to hear from the neophytes and began asking about the process. Was there a time when new seekers were invited to inquire? Whom should they call? How could they get involved? Was there such a thing as "RCIA for Catholics?" It was not that the Easter Vigil had not been celebrated in years past. Of course it had. And the parish previously had an RCIA program. But the year-round process, including the celebration of the liturgical rites throughout the year, and the opportunity to hear the witness of the neophytes touched parishioners deeply. Even though they were fully initiated Catholic Christians, they looked at the RCIA participants and team and in one way or another said, "I want what they have."

Leading for Change, Step 4: Share the Change Vision

Kotter's fourth step of change leadership is to communicate the change vision (87–103). In the example shared above, it is easy to see how the RCIA process itself became the means of communication about the role of the RCIA in forming people for initiation, the call to discipleship and ongoing conversion, and the role each of us has in journeying in faith with one another. The message was shared verbally through the homily (especially in the celebration of the rites and whenever the readings provided an opportunity) and announcements; experientially through Sunday dismissals and rites, especially the Easter Vigil; and through relationship as parishioners experienced the witness and met neophytes socially during the Easter season and beyond it.

What about other aspects of parish life? How can you bring parishioners into the vision, which has been identified, articulated, and for which you have a plan? Kotter identifies seven key points about communication that ensure that people will be likely to embrace the hoped-for change:

- **Keep it simple**. This comes back to clarity of vision. Be prepared to succinctly capture what is changing and why.

- **Use metaphor, analogy, and example**. Make connections with Sacred Scripture (especially the gospels and stories of the early Christian communities), lives of the saints, and the experiences of conversion within the parish community.

- **Employ multiple forums**. Use every means possible to share the message: meetings, bulletin, homily, announcements, and especially relationships! Meet with ministry coordinators and members, parents of children in the parish school or religious education program, teens and their leaders, young adults, and those preparing for sacraments.

- **Repeat, repeat, repeat**. Communicate in all ways, everywhere. Encourage the guiding coalition, pastoral council, clergy, and staff to actively seek ways to share what is in the works and why.

- **Lead by example**. Express enthusiasm. It is okay to acknowledge the challenges that lie ahead—it would be disingenuous not to do so. At the same time, embracing the change and demonstrating one's commitment to do so—even when it requires sacrifice on your part—is essential. "Nothing undermines the communication of a change vision more than behavior on the part of key players that seems inconsistent with the vision" (92).

- **Explain seeming inconsistencies**. Change happens incrementally. While some aspects of the RCIA or parish life might be immediately affected, other elements will not experience change right away. It is good to acknowledge this so that any perceived inconsistencies can be understood by all.

- **Listen and be listened to**. Invite conversation, and listen to the insights, concerns, and ideas of parishioners. Share the big picture when you are able. Learn from what you hear, adjust the plan accordingly, and let people know that the adjustment happened as a result of the ideas they shared.

Engage Everyone

More recently, Kotter has adjusted his change framework to include the importance of "enlisting a volunteer army" at this stage of the process. While we much more readily speak of service and ministry rather than volunteering, and while we do not think of groups of parishioners as an army, Kotter's point is relevant here: draw many people into the change vision so that they become part of the process of bringing it about. Not only are people more likely to accept and embrace change when they hear it from someone they know, the change happens exponentially as the circles of communication widen. People become committed to the change when they see themselves as part of the process.

We return to the recognition that changing the culture of the parish is only possible when many people have been brought into the process. "Lone rangers" are not effective change agents. It takes all of us, reaching out to the people around us, widening our circles, and sharing the story of faith and the vision for change to bring about the transformative life that is possible in the RCIA and the parish.

Questions to Ask Yourself: Sharing the Change Vision

Sharing the change vision for the RCIA: What is your "elevator pitch" in which you succinctly (in three minutes or less) articulate what needs to change and why? What story or experience captures the need for change that you are planning?

Sharing the change vision for the parish: Does your parish have a vision statement? Do parishioners know it and do they understand their part in living it out? What change is anticipated that will bring the vision to life more fully or clearly? What channels of communication exist? How will you employ all of these ways to share the message?

Step 5

Remove Barriers to Your Vision

If the journey of faith in community always took place on a straight path, much of what we have considered thus far would not be necessary, or at the very least, the steps would seem self-evident. Of course, they are not. We might say that this is so by design. God created each of us with the freedom to choose how we will (or if we will) respond to God's love and mercy. The cross of Christ is evidence that even in the most troubling of times, God is with us and invites us into his redemptive plan.

The spiritual life is filled with ups and downs or, as St. Ignatius Loyola observed, consolation and desolation. There are obstacles of our own making and those that are thrust upon us. At times, it seems that God is very near and, in other moments, distant or absent. This is true for everyone who is committed to a living, growing relationship with Christ, including especially those who participate in the RCIA. We who accompany others on this journey will be wise to anticipate moments of spiritual darkness, doubt, and difficulty in accepting the truth of the gospel and church teaching. Likewise, it is important for us to acknowledge obstacles in spiritual growth among parishioners and to ensure that they know they have companions on the journey of faith.

> The secret of everything is to let oneself be carried by God and so carry Him [to others]. (St. John XXIII, in James Martin, SJ, *My Life with the Saints*)

The *Rite of Christian Initiation of Adults* anticipates the need for God's grace throughout the journey of RCIA participants. Minor exorcisms "draw the attention of the catechumens to the real nature of Christian life, the struggle between flesh and spirit, the importance of self-denial for reaching the blessedness of God's kingdom, and the unending need for God's help" (RCIA 90). Blessings are also offered. "The blessings of the catechumens are a sign of God's love and of the Church's tender care. They are bestowed on the catechumens so that, even though they do not as yet have the grace of the sacraments, they may still receive from the Church courage, joy, and peace as they proceed along the difficult journey they have begun" (RCIA 95). These ritual moments reinforce and ask for God's grace in special ways as participants embrace the Christian life.

What obstacles do you often experience in the spiritual life?

What most helps you to overcome these barriers to spiritual growth?

In what ways do you join your life to Christ, especially in suffering, pain, or trial?

In your experience, what obstacles in the spiritual life do RCIA participants experience most often or profoundly?

How do you help them to overcome these spiritual barriers and discern future action?

How do you teach, encourage, and inspire RCIA participants to join their life to Christ?

When Faith Shapes Life, There Are Consequences

Understanding life as a disciple undergoing a process of ongoing conversion helps us to recognize that each day offers opportunities to discern God's will and act on it. Often, daily decisions seem small, yet there is a cumulative effect of all of the choices we make. And of course, some decisions are more substantial and require prayerful discernment over a longer period of time. Placing our daily decisions in the context of faith will be foreign to some as they enter into the RCIA process. For others, the invitation to integrate faith with daily life will be just what they have been looking for. When team members share their own experiences in striving to grow in holiness, they model for participants the ways in which we answer Christ's call in good times and in demanding ones. It is crucial that we remember this and open ourselves to be vulnerable witnesses to all of the ways in which living in faith is experienced in "real life."

The change of life that results from accepting Jesus's call to follow him does not only affect those who participate in the RCIA. Their family, friends, coworkers, and neighbors will see the shifts in priority, behavior, and attitudes that result from participants' growth in faith. Much of the time, the change is welcomed by those who are closest to the seekers. Occasionally, however, family members or good friends may struggle, either due to misperceptions about Catholicism or lack of understanding of the role and effect of faith in their loved one's life. Again, the rite anticipates that such conflict might occur: "Since the Lord in whom they believe is a sign of contradiction, the newly converted often experience divisions and separations, but they also taste the joy that God gives without measure" (RCIA 75.2). It is vital that participants who experience these sorts of divisions have sponsors and others who accompany them with love and care.

The RCIA as Model and Witness

As we have seen in previous chapters, the RCIA stands as witness to and model for the life of conversion in all stages of life and faith. Interactions with participants and team members may spur parishioners to open their minds and hearts to a deeper experience and expression of faith. And while this may be true in any circumstance, it is especially so during times of trial. As parishioners experience the courage and commitment of the RCIA participants to embrace the Christian way of life and find meaning in the cross, they themselves may be urged to do so as well.

Rites such as the scrutinies, the Rite of Calling the Candidates to Continuing Conversion, and the Rite of Election are key moments in the process of conversion for RCIA participants and can also have a powerful impact on parishioners, but only when celebrated in the spirit of the rites. A priest who is a friend once told me that, in his first year as pastor, the Monday after the first scrutiny his phone rang off the hook with people complaining about how those who were preparing for initiation had been called sinners during the scrutiny. It turned out, the previous practice of the parish was to so completely water down the language of the rite that the point of it had been lost. The following Sunday, his homily included catechesis on the scrutiny and an explanation that we are all sinners in need of conversion! "In the liturgy and liturgical catechesis of Lent the reminder of baptism already received or the preparation for its reception, as well as the theme of repentance, renew the entire community along with those being prepared to celebrate the paschal mystery" (RCIA 138).

Change: What and Why

Obstacles and barriers are inevitable in the spiritual life and in the life of the parish. We have glimpsed aspects of the dynamics of change in the spiritual life, and it will be good for us to also acknowledge some of the potential barriers to change within the parish. What we consider here will not eliminate obstacles, but we will plan to manage them when they emerge—personally, with the seekers who take part in the RCIA, and in the parish.

Change is rarely easy. Sometimes, it is just the process of shifting from one mind-set to another that takes time. At other moments, it is the change in practice that is challenging as people have to adjust and learn new ways. There are other times in which it is the people that become obstacles to the intended change. They aren't really ready, or are not on board, or are threatened by a change in role or responsibility that is part of the change plan. Whatever the reason, it is important to name what is or is not happening and create strategies to remove the obstacles or barriers or be prepared for the change to never take root.

It is helpful to anticipate possible resistance or obstacles when implementing a plan that involves change, and unless you plan to remain exactly as you are, any plan will inevitably include change. Having named the barriers, the plan can include strategies for addressing them from the start. Even with this, however, other obstacles will likely emerge as you take the first steps toward change. Then, you must be prepared to adapt in order to ensure that the plan is not derailed. This is true in our personal spiritual lives, in the experience of the RCIA participants, and with our plans to adjust the way the RCIA is enacted and the way the life of the parish is shaped.

Leading for Change, Step 5: Remove Barriers to Your Vision

Kotter's next step in the change framework is to remove barriers and empower broad-based action (105–119). At first glance, the six steps that he has identified make perfect sense for an RCIA process. There are insights in the steps below that are applicable to the spiritual life as well. Let us explore his steps from both perspectives. We will walk through the steps first as we plan to make changes in the way the RCIA is carried out. Following this exploration, we will apply the steps in relationship to our life of faith where they are applicable.

Six steps to remove barriers and empower broad-based action

1. Empower (entrust) people (with responsibility) to effect change.

2. Communicate a sensible vision.

3. Make structures compatible with the vision.

4. Provide formation and training.

5. Align systems with the vision.

6. Pastorally confront those who undercut needed change. (Kotter, 119, adapted)

Empower People to Effect Change

Change is needed. You know why it is so and what needs to change. You have articulated this with a sense of urgency and have a plan to make the change a reality. Now, people need to have the authority or ability to put the change into effect. This seems so clear, and yet, it is not uncommon to have a plan in place and never move to the next step of actually enacting the plan. And often, the breakdown happens at this step.

Let's say for a moment that the guiding coalition—along with the pastor and other parish leaders—has created a plan to move to year-round RCIA process. Your vision team has communicated the compelling need. Members of the coalition have talked with RCIA team members, liturgy committee members, and those responsible for music ministry. Announcements have been made, and rooms have been set aside on the parish calendar. But when the Rite of Acceptance into the Order of Catechumens is scheduled at a time of the year that is different from what would have been in the past, questions arise. Who authorized this change, the RCIA coordinator is asked. Does this mean that the people who participate in the rite will be baptized this year or next? Suddenly, the RCIA coordinator feels on the defensive. Had the plan not been communicated well enough? Was there some misunderstanding about the timeline for implementation? Does she have the authority to carry out the plan, or does she need to go back for permission?

Questions are sure to arise as change is implemented, and the more we can anticipate the questions the better. But there is something else at work in the example above. Once the plan is in place, those responsible for carrying out the plan must be given the authority to do so. Healthy conversations and dialogue may be involved, yet they must happen in a spirit of collaboration, and ultimately, those who are responsible for implementing the plan must be allowed to do so. At this stage in change management, designated leaders must have the authority to enact the change plan. Those who are responsible must also be given the ability to take risks in developing new processes or carrying out the plans that have been developed. Otherwise, the fear of failure can become an obstacle to change.

There is an additional nuance that I believe is helpful at this stage, and it is about the word "empowerment." I remember talking with my pastor quite a few times in those first tenuous moments as we began to make the needed changes at the parish. One day, after speaking about what was going to happen, the pastor began to say that we needed to empower those who would implement the plan. Then he stopped and said that he had been thinking about that word, "empowerment," because servant leadership is not about power. It is, however, carried out in a relationship of trust. Responsibility is entrusted to us, and we fulfill our responsibilities by using the gifts that have been entrusted to us by our good and gracious God. In what ways are people entrusted with responsibility to effect change?

Communicate a Sensible Vision

We have spoken much about the need for vision, but this step adds an important element to the process. The vision must be sensible. This means that if the change that is anticipated is substantial or complex, it is best to communicate the vision in smaller stages.

Perhaps you can communicate the vision as a multifaceted process or tell people that the changes will be happening gradually over a period of time. This step also encourages us to look at what we are planning from the perspective of all involved, including those who are not involved in parish ministry. Is what we are planning sensible? We must ensure that we aim high, without being pie-in-the-sky.

This raises probably the most prevalent obstacle to change that is found in parish life: "We've always done it this way." When parishioners or staff understand the change vision as not only necessary but sensible, it is reasonable to expect that they will get beyond the idea that change cannot, should not, or will not happen. It is necessary to anticipate the "we've always done it this way" response by thinking about the change from the perspective of those who will be affected. Do they understand the need for change and urgency about it? Have they been engaged in the planning? Have they been given opportunities to offer their ideas and suggestions? Have they been formed and trained well so that they are equipped to carry out the plan (see below)? When people are drawn into a sensible vision, "we've always done it this way" can give way to "let's give it a try."

Make Structures Compatible with the Vision

Let's imagine a parish in which the RCIA process has previously been a series of meetings with the pastor or a deacon. The plan is to move to a process through which an RCIA coordinator and team will enact the process. It is essential that the coordinator and team know "where they fit" in the parish structure. If the coordinator is a staff person, have his or her other responsibilities been evaluated to ensure that he or she can attend to the process well? Is there a budget for training, formation, and resources? If the coordinator is a parishioner minister, to whom does she or he consult for guidance? What authority does she or he have to carry out the process?

Provide Formation and Training

This step is connected to the ones above and takes them a step further. Everyone who is in any way connected to the intended change needs formation and training so that they can carry it out well. This requires forethought and planning so that those who will implement the change plan are assured that they are ready and equipped for what lies ahead.

Align Systems with the Vision

This is another crucial step that is often overlooked in parish life and is similar to the point above about structure. We may say we want change but do nothing to change the structure that surrounds the change. Go back to the idea of moving to a year-round RCIA process. This will likely necessitate a larger team, or current team members may need to shift responsibilities in order to make the change possible. Yet, we may worry about adding people to the team or overcommitting those who are already part of it. So the change does not happen or it stumbles along. Another key example: the RCIA is a process of formation and evangelization. Yet how often do we speak with those who answer the phone to help them understand this? Or those who greet people at the doors of church? Or those who are responsible for children's catechesis? Unless all of these people understand the importance of welcoming and have a good sense of the ways in which the process is carried out, there will surely be missteps and missed opportunities.

Pastorally Confront Those Who Undercut Needed Change

Obviously, this is a sensitive topic! The reality is that occasionally a person stands as an obstacle to the implementation of the change plan. That person might not be doing so purposefully. He or she may simply not understand or does not feel ready and needs formation or training in order to do what needs to be done. It is possible, however, that the person has made up his or her mind that the change is not needed, and as far as he or she is concerned, that is that. What is necessary in this situation is an honest, forthright conversation in which the change vision is explained, questions and concerns are brought to light, and the person is encouraged to get on board. If not, the person's involvement must be curtailed. Perhaps a new ministry needs his or her service, or a break is in order.

This is especially difficult when the person involved is a parishioner. I find that one of the main obstacles to change in parishes is the concern that parishioner ministers will be upset. It is quite common to hear people ask, "How can you 'fire' a volunteer?" This brings us back to the need for formation and training and the shared understanding of servant leadership and ministry. My experience is that when parishes regularly gather those who serve for formation, many of these sorts of issues are minimized. When parishioners are led to grow in understanding of themselves as disciples who serve Christ and the church, they give of themselves willingly. They can also be formed to see that the ministry of which they are a part is an aspect of the life of the church, connected to all of the other ministries and elements of parish life. With this recognition, it is much more likely to find parishioners ready for give-and-take in order to be part of a change for the better.

Removing Barriers to Foster Conversion in the Spiritual Life

Forming People to Effect Change

Are we prepared to embrace a life of ongoing conversion, and are we ready to help others to do so as well? Often, when seekers arrive they do not have language or experience in living faith that makes it possible for them to understand the life of discipleship as a process of change. This happens in time, and as it does, we can form them to be open to conversion as part and parcel of the life of discipleship. It is not so much that we are "empowering" ourselves or others for change as much as we are helping one another to anticipate change as a necessary and meaningful aspect of following Christ with our lives.

Communicate a Sensible Vision

While it might be argued that the Christian life is not "sensible," in that it should entail a radical movement toward God and living Christ's way of love, keeping that vision in front of ourselves and those we accompany is crucial to the process of conversion. What does it "look like" to live as a disciple? What does this mean in daily life? While some teaching may seem theological or abstract, it is crucial that our primary focus is the essential foundation of faith in Jesus Christ.

> We must not think that in catechesis the kerygma gives way to a supposedly more "solid" formation. Nothing is more solid, profound, secure, meaningful and wisdom-filled than that initial proclamation. All Christian formation consists of entering more deeply into the kerygma, which is reflected in and constantly illumines, the work of catechesis, thereby enabling us to understand more fully the significance of every subject which the latter treats. It is the message capable of responding to the desire for the infinite which abides in every human heart. (Joy of the Gospel, 165)

Making Structures Compatible with the Vision and Aligning Systems with It

While this does not correspond as readily to the notion of spiritual growth, there is something that is essential here: we hold the vision of living and growing as Christian people in front of ourselves, and we measure everything alongside that vision. We know "where" we want to go—we are journeying in a relationship with God, toward the fullness of life in Christ—and we are continually discerning how we are called to shape our lives accordingly. The obstacles we encounter must be acknowledged and future action discerned in order to grow in holiness. This life is ideal, and yet it is an ideal that is attainable.

Provide Formation and Training

How are parishioners, including RCIA participants and team members, formed to understand that change is an essential aspect of living as a disciple?

Pastorally Confront Those Who Undercut Needed Change

This seems to be at the crux of all we have explored in this chapter about obstacles and barriers in the spiritual life. What within us holds us back from following Christ more nearly? Is there a person or group that stands as a barrier to spiritual growth? Are there habits that must change? What about those we accompany? What barriers or obstacles do they face? How will you journey with them as they place their trust in God with their hearts and lives?

Questions to Ask Yourself: Remove Barriers to Your Vision

What stands out in all that we have explored together in this chapter in relationship to your own personal spiritual life, that of your RCIA team and participants, and the life of your parish?

What steps will you take to let go of what holds you back?

Step 6

Celebrate Progress toward Your Vision

In the previous chapter, we explored the many obstacles that may impede our progress— spiritually, pastorally, and practically. Yet, all is not darkness, frustration, and challenge, and gratefully so. While we are wise to be mindful of potential pitfalls on the journey, it is also important to notice and celebrate positive steps along the way. Without attentiveness to growth, our energy and commitment will likely wane. It is difficult to continue to work toward an ongoing goal, be it the life of discipleship or the processes we put in place to encourage living faith, if we do not see signs that we are on the right track.

> Finally, [beloved], whatever is true, whatever is honorable, whatever is just, whatever is pure, whatever is lovely, whatever is gracious, if there is any excellence and if there is anything worthy of praise, think about these things. Keep on doing what you have learned and received and heard and seen in me. Then the God of peace will be with you. (Phil 4:8-9)

Celebrating Steps on the Path of Change

John called just after Easter one year, inquiring about the RCIA process and what was involved in preparing for baptism. He had been a member of the community with his wife and children for many years, but it was only recently that he had begun to open his heart to Jesus and to consider the possibility of baptism for himself. He was unsure at first, but as weeks turned into months, he grew in certainty that he was ready to respond to the yearnings in his heart and to follow Jesus Christ with his life.

It was only after John participated in the Rite of Acceptance into the Order of Catechumens that we began to understand the impact his journey was having on his family and friends. His wife shared how she had prayed for him since they met, hoping that he would open his heart to God in time. Friends talked about the changes they were experiencing with John and how his growing faith inspired them in their commitment to Christ. We began to recognize that John's growing faith was touching people who were not his friends as well. Since he had been involved in service projects, came to social events, and often attended Mass with his family, parishioners felt connected to him in a special way. Now, as John was dismissed from the Sunday assembly, people noticed. They asked him what had led him to consider baptism and begin the RCIA process. He enthusiastically shared his experience with the parishioners and told us how moving it was to know that so many in the community were praying for him and all of the participants.

When the time came for John and the other catechumens who were ready to celebrate the Rite of Election, it became clear that this group of participants had touched the hearts of many parishioners. People stopped me in the grocery store to assure me of their prayers. Others lingered after Mass, eager to share how they were inspired to open their hearts to God in new or deeper ways as a result of the participants' witness. Lent, with the celebrations of the scrutinies and presentations of the Lord's Prayer and the Creed, was not only a season of purification and enlightenment for the elect but for the entire community. The Easter Vigil that year was the most widely attended in the life of the parish up to that point in time; throughout the season of Easter, parishioners spoke about the ways their lives were changing for the better. At Pentecost, we invited a few of the newly initiated to speak at the beginning of the Sunday liturgies, sharing a small glimpse of their faith journey, their gratitude for the prayers and support of the community, and their commitment to live as disciples. New seekers arrived; parishioners participated in faith formation opportunities to a greater extent. The community was changed. While we were aware of many aspects of the RCIA process and the life of the parish that needed further attention, we could clearly point to many examples of transformation and know that none of us would ever be the same again.

The Rites as Markers and Inspiration

What we experienced in the time that John and his companions journeyed through the catechumenate helped us understand more fully the impact of the RCIA on the wider parish community. The rites, which celebrate spiritual progress for the participants, also act as markers and inspiration for the team and parishioners. The rites of the RCIA provide a regular rhythm of moments through which all in the parish may recognize the role of faith in their lives. We can think of the rites as offering the impetus for people to reflect and to discern future direction for spiritual growth. Let us consider this together by highlighting the primary public movements and rites of the catechumenate and a sampling of questions each may evoke for team members and parishioners.

The Rite of Acceptance into the Order of Catechumens

In the Rite of Acceptance, those who are ready to enter the catechumenate "express and the Church accepts their intention to respond to God's call to follow the way of Christ" (RCIA, Outline for Christian Initiation of Adults). As the catechumens publicly declare their desire to grow in faith and are marked with the cross of Christ, we who are present may be drawn to ask ourselves what is the role of faith in our daily lives. In what ways have we made a commitment to be formed as God's people, as disciples of Jesus Christ? How does the presence of the catechumens remind us that we are called to share our faith with others?

Dismissal from the Sunday Assembly

Each Sunday, catechumens are "kindly dismissed" at the conclusion of the Liturgy of the Word (RCIA 75.3). Those who are gathered promise their prayers and support as the catechumens are sent out to reflect on what they have heard and experienced and to allow Christ to influence their lives. In what ways do our ongoing prayers for those in the RCIA process remind us of our call to be with one another in community? How are we shaped by word and sacrament?

Sending to the Rite of Election

While most in the parish do not have the opportunity to participate in the Rite of Election, the sending ritual gives everyone an opportunity to reflect on who we are and are called to be in God's sight. In what ways do we understand ourselves as the elect of God? What does it mean to be created in God's image and called to holiness?

Scrutinies

During the season of Lent, those who are preparing for initiation celebrate the scrutinies, "rites for self-searching and repentance" (RCIA 141). Together, we reflect on the gospel narratives of the woman at the well, the man who was blind from birth, and the raising of Lazarus. In these crucial weeks of purification and enlightenment, we commit ourselves to *metanoia*, life-changing transformation in Christ, and we ask ourselves: From what must we turn away? How will we turn back to God and God's ways? For what do we thirst? How does faith give us sight? Is Christ our light and life?

Sacraments of Initiation

At the great Easter Vigil, we initiate the elect and draw closer to the risen Lord. In the celebration of baptism, confirmation, and Eucharist, we are again immersed in the saving, merciful love of God; renew our awareness and desire for the power of the Holy Spirit in our hearts and lives; and feast on the Body and Blood of Christ. As the elect are initiated into Christ's body, we ask ourselves: What does it mean to be baptized into Christ, who is Priest, Prophet, and King? In what ways do we listen and respond to the Holy Spirit? What difference does it make that we are nourished by and drawn to Christ and to the community as members of Christ's body?

Mystagogy

Throughout the Easter season, we invite the neophytes to explore the mysteries of God's love and the implications of their participation in the sacred mysteries as fully initiated Christian people. This exploration is for us as well. In fact, all of the Christian life might be considered "mystagogy."

> In the broader sense, mystagogy represents the Christian's lifelong education and formation in the faith. By analogy it signifies the continuous character of catechesis in the life of the Christian. Conversion to Christ is a lifelong process that should be accompanied at every stage by a vital catechesis that leads Christians on their journey towards holiness. (*National Directory for Catechesis*, 35)

What practices of prayer, formation, communal life, and service help us to reflect upon and live as Christian people throughout the stages of our lives as disciples?

Change: What and Why

In previous chapters, we have noted the importance of accompanying relationships in the spiritual life. When we share the journey of faith with others, we help one another to discern the ways in which we are called to live, grow, and act as Christian disciples in the world. Discernment is a communal endeavor. It is more than an individual person feeling called to do something. Whether through spiritual direction, in small faith communities, with peer-to-peer mentors, or in faith-filled friendships or family relationships, we listen for the voice of the Lord and commit ourselves to specific action as a result. With a trusted spiritual companion, we find the strength and wisdom needed to weather the difficult moments and to overcome obstacles along the way. We also recognize God's grace, moments of deepening faith, and experiences of God's mercy and forgiveness.

Remember Acts 2:42, RCIA 75, and the Introduction to *Our Hearts Were Burning Within Us*? Each points to common aspects of the life of faith: worship, community, word, and service. In the words of the RCIA,

> The instruction that the catechumens receive during this [the catechumenate] period should be of a kind that while presenting Catholic teaching in its entirety also enlightens faith, directs the heart toward God, fosters participation in the liturgy, inspires apostolic activity, and nurtures a life completely in accord with the spirit of Christ. (78)

As we journey with others in community, we become adept at watching for, listening to, and recognizing signs of maturing faith in our own lives and among RCIA participants, team members, and parishioners. Being attentive to the ways in which we are growing as individuals and within the community encourages and strengthens us for future growth as committed people of faith.

In our accompanying relationships with one another, we may use the categories of worship, community, word, and service to discern areas for greater attention and lived faith response. We encourage one another to enter fully into liturgical prayer and to develop regular patterns of personal prayer; we participate to a greater extent in the life of the faith community and come to know one another as family; we grow in appreciation for church teaching and its implications in our lives; we urge each other to offer service, grow in solidarity with others, especially the poor, and to develop a true spirit of generosity in response to God's lavish love. These actions are universal manifestations of a maturing relationship with God in Christ Jesus.

We Are Never Finished!

We are never finished disciples. Regardless of our age or stage in life and faith, we are called to turn to God and follow Jesus. While in other processes of change the focus is often on what more there is to do, spiritual growth is not always about more as in more tasks to do, efforts to be made, or things we need to learn, although there will at times be more that needs to be done. Ongoing conversion is about deepening our relationship with God, joining ourselves with Christ as witnesses to and bearers of Christ's love in the world, and growing as people who rely on the presence of the Holy Spirit. This life of ongoing conversion has spiritual and practical implications for each of us. Simply knowing that the call to discipleship is a life-long endeavor is not enough. We need markers or occasional points throughout the moments, seasons, and years of our lives in which we acknowledge the ways in which faith is, or is not, influencing the way we live. Just as we must be prepared for and manage the times in which we face barriers and obstacles on the path of discipleship, we must also celebrate the times of grace and growth in faith.

Leading for Change, Step 6:
Celebrate Progress toward Your Vision

Kotter's next step in the change process is to generate short-term wins (121–135). In other words, it may be all well and good to know that it will take time to fully realize our vision. However, it is not realistic to forge ahead without glimmers of that vision in progress. While we know that the process of discipleship is a lifelong endeavor, it is important to plan for and celebrate the signs of growth along the way. This has both personal and pastoral implications.

The role of short-term wins

- Provide evidence that sacrifices are worth it: Wins greatly help justify the short-term costs involved.
- Reward change agents with a pat on the back: After a lot of hard work, positive feedback builds morale and motivation.

- Help fine-tune vision and strategies: Short-term wins give the guiding coalition concrete data on the viability of their ideas.

- Undermine cynics and self-serving resisters: Clear improvements in performance make it difficult for people to block needed change.

- Keep bosses on board: Provides those higher in the hierarchy with evidence that the transformation is on track.

- Build momentum: Turns neutrals into supporters, reluctant supporters into active helpers. (Kotter, 127)

Celebrating Progress in Parish Life

As we create our plan for change in the RCIA or the parish, it is important that we identify specific steps toward our long-term goal. Not only will this ensure that we will make progress, it also provides a means for recognizing progress as it is experienced. This is essential. The guiding coalition and those who implement the plan need to sense that their efforts are starting to have an impact. Kotter explains that without such incremental "wins" or points of movement toward the vision, the change effort will wane and often fail. Not only are such signs of progress encouraging, these steps along the path provide key feedback necessary to fine-tune the vision and strategies that are part of the plan.

Let's say that the RCIA coordinator, team, and the parish faith formation director have decided to offer a few opportunities for adults in the parish to gather with the RCIA participants for prayer, faith sharing, and learning throughout the year. They identify dates, plan the gatherings, and promote the opportunities through the usual channels, but also focus on personal invitations to encourage participation. The first gathering is an Advent evening of reflection, and while many worried that few would attend because December is such a busy month for most people, the church is nicely filled and people offer many positive comments. The reception and feedback encourage the planning team and those who participated to personally invite others to join them for the Lenten soup and service evening. While the goal of greater commitment to discipleship among parishioners is long term, these short-term steps provide encouragement for the planning team, feedback from participants, and momentum for future gatherings and strategies for adult faith formation.

Attentiveness to Spiritual Growth

As with the previous step in the change process, the concept of "short-term wins" is not precisely transferable to the spiritual life. Yet, there is something important for us to consider in this step, and that is to be attentive to spiritual growth as we journey in faith. Obstacles and barriers cannot be missed. We easily recognize the challenges to accepting Christ's call and responding with our lives. Ongoing reflection also leads us to acknowledge and address spiritual complacency. What we may miss, however, are signs that we are changing, that our lives are being shaped by the grace of God, that we are growing toward holiness.

Questions to Ask Yourself: Celebrate Progress toward Your Vision

Celebrate Progress toward Your Vision: RCIA or Parish Plan

Consider the draft plan that is emerging through your discussions as you read this book. What incremental steps have you identified? How will you recognize progress toward your vision? Be sure to schedule occasional moments to assess positive steps, acknowledge points for further attention, and make adjustments in the plan as needed.

Celebrate Personal Spiritual Growth

What signs help you to recognize spiritual growth in yourself or others? Do you take moments to recognize the ways in which you have grown or are growing in your relationship with God and are living as a follower of Jesus?

Keep Your Vision Alive

Where are we? Where are we going? We might be tempted to think that we are finished at this point. If you have already put an initial plan in place, you may have seen good progress toward your vision. Many may have contributed to bringing it to reality in their lives as disciples, in the RCIA process, and in the parish. If you are identifying initial first steps, you know what needs to be done to begin the process of transformation.

Yet, even when we see signs of growth, development, and progress toward our goals, we know we will never fully reach our vision of a community of disciples who embrace lifelong conversion. While the RCIA process may effectively bring the vision of the rite to life, the arrival of new participants inherently brings challenges and joys along the way. Likewise, the programs and processes that are established within the parish may serve well for a time, yet consistent discernment for future action is necessary.

Beginning in conversion, change of mind and heart, this commitment is expressed not in a single action, nor even in a number of actions over a period of time, but in an entire way of life. It means committing one's very self to the Lord. (USCCB, Stewardship: A Disciple's Response, 2)

With progress made toward the vision we have established, our attention begins to shift to the long term. Even though positive steps have been taken, now is not the time to relax. With a few obstacles behind us and some progress to celebrate, it is time to learn from our early experience and to build strategies for lasting, sustainable change.

The Liturgical Year: Our Operating Principle

Earlier in this book, we spoke of the many "moving parts" that must be taken into consideration in leading people to lifelong conversion in Christ. The complexity of many facets of life in the parish requires leaders to be consistently attentive, patient, and tenacious. As we begin to plan for long-term transformation, we must find a way to lead for and manage change within the complex web of people, processes, and parish life in order to engage people in a life of discipleship.

In chapter 3, we briefly noted the way in which the liturgical cycle of Sundays, seasons, and feasts provide an ongoing immersion into the paschal mystery. Now, let's return to the centrality of the liturgy as the "summit toward which the activity of the Church is directed" and the "fount from which all her power flows" (Constitution on the Sacred Liturgy, 10). Through participation in the Sunday Eucharist and daily and seasonal prayer, devotions, spiritual reading, and practices, we are drawn deeply into the mystery of God's love, invited to become immersed in this mystery, and respond to it with our lives. The rhythm of the liturgical year provides the foundation for lifelong conversion in Christ.

The liturgy is central to our spiritual lives as Catholic Christians, to be sure. There are practical implications for us to consider here as well. Much of parish life is already focused on Sunday Mass and the sacramental life of the church. In most parishes, there are activities that are particular to a liturgical season, such as Lenten soup suppers and Stations of the Cross. Other aspects of parish life simply happen without much reflection on the way they are or are not aligned with the liturgical year. As a result, we miss opportunities to lead people toward a way of life that fully integrates their faith into the days, months, seasons, and years of their lives.

With the above in mind, let us think of the liturgy as the operating principle for parish life. When we organize the life of the parish through the lens of the liturgical cycle of Sundays and seasons, all of the various strands of prayer, programs, processes, and practices fit together, practically and spiritually. Practically, we do not need to add layers of activity that are extraneous to the season. Rather, we may find ways to celebrate the seasons more deeply. Advent is Advent, with its spirit of waiting and anticipation; Christmas is Christmas, in its joyful recognition of the mystery of the incarnation. As I have talked with parish leaders about this, I often see signs of relief in their faces, especially pastors. Not only does organizing parish life through and around the liturgical seasons make practical sense, it makes spiritual sense for our people. When our programs flow from the liturgy and are aligned with the spirit of the liturgical seasons, people are led to deeper reflection on the meaning of the season in their lives.

Look at your parish calendar for the coming month. Are there activities that seem to not fit with the current liturgical season? Would there be a better time of year for a particular initiative or program?

Change: What and Why

With the liturgical year as our operating principle, we can ensure that people, processes, and the parish will be led to ongoing growth in discipleship within the community of faith. Our plans to foster transformation can be sustained. Now it is time to think very practically about how this can be accomplished.

Leading for and Managing Change

Throughout this book, I have used the phrase "leading for and managing change." It is now time to make a distinction between these two dimensions, leadership and management. Volumes have been written about both, and we will keep our exploration here very simple. Those who lead work with others to cast a compelling vision and develop structures that will ensure that the vision can become reality. Managers are responsible for specific elements of the organization and bring the vision to life within the realm of their responsibility.

In parishes, the formal and informal leaders (pastor, staff, and pastoral council) discern the vision and ensure that coordinators of ministries and groups (managers) understand the vision and have what is needed to bring it to life. In order to create an environment in which people, processes, and the parish thrive, it is essential that we both lead for and manage change on an ongoing basis.

A Little Structure Goes a Long Way

This is a point of struggle for many parishes. Remember our previous exploration of the painful process of planning? Most often, the pain results from plans that are created but are only minimally implemented, if at all. In speaking with parish groups, I find that the breakdown is a result of lack of clarity, direction, or structure necessary to put the plan into action. Those who were involved in developing the plan understand the reasons for it, and they believe that by sharing the plan, it will be implemented. Others who were not part of the planning process often see a disconnection, however. They may know that a plan exists but do not understand their role in carrying it out. In other words, leaders have cast the vision and perhaps have communicated the vision to others, but managers, the coordinators of ministries and groups, do not have sufficient direction, materials, or authority to carry out their portion of the plan.

This is challenging for a number of reasons. First, the "managers," coordinators of ministries and groups, are people who selflessly offer their time in response to the call to serve. They are usually volunteers—unpaid people whose service is essential and offered in addition to the responsibilities of family and work. Second, many of the "leaders" are also volunteers who serve in the capacity of a term on the pastoral council or other guiding group. Third, many of the people who are serving are not part of only one ministry or group. They rely on each other and staff when one exists to keep everything in motion. Add to this a new process or change an existing one, and we can easily see why clarity and direction are so important.

In the short term of the initial processes of change, it is possible to succeed through the efforts of a small group of people. The guiding coalition may involve a few others, and early steps are accomplished. Sometimes, this is necessary in order for others to grasp the potential of the greater vision. For the longer term, however, the leaders—pastor, staff, council, and vision team—need to develop a structure or ensure that existing structures function effectively to make future transformation possible and sustainable. This does not mean that we need to create more complex systems through which the complexity of parish life is managed! As in all organizations, parishes include many interdependent dimensions. We need only develop enough structure to manage what we are called to accomplish. No more, no less.

Structure enables the many parishioner council members, coordinators, and members of ministries to have the materials and authority to effectively carry out the plan. The structure also provides a means for quickly assessing progress toward a goal or objective and for celebrating what is accomplished through the service of all. Here is the rub: providing a structure through which coordinators, ministries, and groups have what they need to carry out their part of the plan is only possible when leaders give them the authority and freedom to act. This only happens when those who serve together are ready and willing to collaborate with each other.

We're All in This Together

As people who are in communion with Christ and one another, we serve together, valuing the contribution each may make as members of Christ's body.

> An ecclesiology of communion looks upon different gifts and functions not as adversarial but as enriching and complementary. It appreciates the Church's unity as an expression of the mutual and reciprocal gifts brought into harmony by the Holy Spirit. An ecclesiology of communion recognizes diversity in unity and acknowledges the Spirit as the source of all the gifts that serve to build up Christ's Body. (USCCB, Co-Workers in the Vineyard of the Lord, 20)

In speaking with people who are involved in their parishes, what I often hear is far from the ideal of such an ecclesiology of communion. Coordinators of ministry often keep their circles of involvement small, trusting only a few friends to serve with them. Leaders often say they want everyone involved but micromanage the details, limiting opportunities for people to make a genuine contribution. Pastors and staff sometimes moan about the scarce number of people who are willing to give of themselves in substantial ways, yet, in the same breath, they itemize the ways in which parishioner involvement is complicated and sometimes falls short of expectations. Small. Limited. Scarce. When we fail to trust one another to carry out the portions of the plan entrusted to us, the parish and its people are less likely to grow, thrive, and be transformed. Collaboration in ministry is necessary and life-giving and requires commitment on the part of each person and group. It takes all of us doing what we can to bring our vision of discipleship in community to life. We must be committed to serve together, recognizing that each person has a unique and valuable contribution to make. Genuine collaboration in ministry is necessary to sustain ongoing transformation in the lives of people, processes, and the parish.

Leading for Change, Step 7: Keep Your Vision Alive

Kotter's seventh step is to sustain momentum and acceleration (137–151). In his work with organizational transformation, he has found that one of the greatest pitfalls is to prematurely let up on energy and focus during the change process. While it is important to generate and celebrate short-term progress, it is also essential to be clear that more change is necessary. "Whenever you let up before the job is done, critical momentum can be lost and regression may follow" (137).

What step 7 looks like in a successful, major change effort

- **More change, not less**: The guiding coalition uses the credibility afforded by short-term progress to tackle additional and bigger change projects.

- **More help**: Additional people are brought in and developed to help with all the changes.

- **Leadership**: Senior people focus on maintaining clarity of shared purpose for the overall effort and keeping urgency levels up.

- **Management and leadership from within**: Coordinators and those involved provide leadership for and manage specific initiatives within the larger plan for change.

- **Reduction of unnecessary interdependencies**: To make change easier in both the short and long term, coordinators identify unnecessary duplication of effort and eliminate it. (Kotter, 150, adapted)

Questions to Ask Yourself:
Building a Sustainable Plan

Take time to carefully develop a plan that will ensure lasting change and conversion in Christ among people, processes, and the parish. Make sure your plan answers these questions:

- Why is change needed?

- What needs to happen?

- How will the change process be communicated to the community?

- Who will implement each facet of the change plan?

- How will the plan be enacted?

- What resources (people, materials) are needed?

- How will the gifts and talents of people be called forth in genuine contribution?

- How will you measure the impact of the change over time?

- How will you discern future direction once the initial changes have been carried out?

Step 8

Make Your Vision Last

Imagine for a moment that all of your plans for change have been fulfilled and that for a period of time the people, RCIA process, and parish are journeying well on the path of ongoing conversion as disciples. People readily speak about the impact of faith in their daily lives, the challenge of responding to Christ's call, and their commitment to give of themselves for others. RCIA team members accompany participants, help them embrace the Gospel, and celebrate milestone rites, which also encourages parishioners toward lifelong transformation. The parish has processes to form people in faith at all ages and stages of life, parishioners make meaningful contributions to the parish, work for justice, advocate for peace, and give in the wider community. All of this is accomplished through growing recognition that all are drawn to communion with Christ and one another.

This is not a vague, never-to-be-fulfilled dream. It can happen, and does, in parishes of all sizes, shapes, and demographics. You may experience some version of this vision come to life in your parish. And yet, it will not last. Not because you have not done your work well or because someone failed to hold up his or her end of the process. It will not last because it is not meant to last. At least not in a definitive, "we made it!" sort of manner. Rather, by definition, communities of disciples who embrace transformation in Christ will always change. This is the point of this book.

Naming That for Which We Aim

Before proceeding, it will be helpful to recall the elements of the vision we have identified.

The People

- Growing in holiness and reaching out to others with God's love
- Actively cultivating a lively baptismal and eucharistic spirituality with a powerful sense of mission and apostolate
- Living as disciples in their homes, places of work, parish, and the world
- Embracing lifelong conversion as an essential dimension of discipleship

The RCIA

- A process of and catalyst for conversion, change of mind and heart, among participants and team members
- Witnesses and calls people to a deep relationship with Jesus Christ
- Evangelizes and forms participants, team members, and the wider parish community

The Parish

- A community of disciples on a journey of lifelong transformation
- The "home and school of communion"
- Vitally alive in faith

A Culture of Conversion

What a powerful vision to set before ourselves! Ensuring that the people, processes, and parish will always have this vision of lifelong conversion in community as their frame of reference is a dynamic process that requires consistent attention and action. This is about more than a series of things or steps. It is about the establishment of a culture through which the parish and its people carry out the mission of Christ in the church and in the world.

> Culture refers to norms of behavior and shared values among a group of people. Norms of behavior are common or pervasive ways of acting that are found in a group and that persist because group members tend to behave in ways that teach these practices to new members, rewarding those who fit in and sanctioning those who do not. Shared values are important concerns and goals shared by most of the people in a group that tend to shape group behavior and that often persist over time even when group membership changes. (Kotter, 156)

While in organizations such as businesses, nonprofits, and schools initial changes happen and often remain at the behavioral level, we have first focused on shared values, rooted in our Catholic theology and the vision that emerges from the *Rite of Christian Initiation of Adults* and other church documents. With the vision firmly in our minds and hearts, we can discern the behaviors, practices, and actions that are necessary to bring the vision to life.

Our Shared Vision: Discipleship.
The New Norm: Lifelong Conversion.

We have been establishing the vision of a culture in which people, the RCIA process, and the parish itself embrace a life of ongoing change, growing in holiness, following the model and example of Jesus Christ through the power of the Holy Spirit. If what has preceded this chapter has seemed overwhelming at times, it is because this is such a great vision for which to aim.

The Invisible Influence of Culture

It is important to recognize that much of the influence of culture is invisible or nearly so. We do not see or perceive the culture, but it helps to shape us. Every culture bears attitudes, assumptions, and behavioral expectations, subtly communicated through personal interaction between members of the community. Consider your previous exploration of the powerful impact of relationships and you will grasp the ways in which the behavioral norms of culture are spread. That is why the steps we have explored in this book are so crucial. All organizations, including our parishes, have a culture, intentionally so or not. When we consider it in this way, it becomes clear that forming people, processes, and parishes to follow Christ's continual call to conversion is necessary. If we do not do this, we will be shaped, less profoundly, less intentionally, with far less transformation and impact.

I liken this process of becoming a part of a parish or ministry to welcoming someone into our family. In the past few years, my husband and I have celebrated the marriage of both of our young adult children. I watched them bring their now-spouses to family gatherings for the first time. Our son first brought his girlfriend to a family reunion. He introduced her to family members, shared family stories with her, and rarely left her side for the initial hours of the visit. Only when she was comfortable did he leave for a few minutes, making sure she was enjoying conversation with a group of cousins before going to the snack table and returning with a plate of goodies for her. Without being taught to do this, our son knew how to introduce his friend to the family. And without saying it, he was beginning the process of inculturating her into the family. Through his actions and the stories he shared, he conveyed what it means to be a part of the family, why the family is important to him, the experiences that have helped to shape him. And he was inviting her in, hoping that she would become part of the family over time.

Reflect on this from your own experience. Think about your participation as a member of the RCIA team or another parish ministry. How did you become connected? Were you invited, or did you offer your service? How were you welcomed? Was there specific training or onboarding that helped you understand expectations and to be familiar with how things are done? Did you learn from a book, resource, or people? How would you describe what it means to be a part of this ministry? What is the impact on you and on participants? It is likely that even with some formal training, much of what you have learned about the RCIA or parish life and have passed on to others was communicated person to person, through words and actions.

Change: What and Why

Changing culture is a long process precisely because so much of the culture is experienced and expressed unconsciously. The process of culture change is about aligning actions and attitudes with our shared vision. We may have a clear vision and have a plan to move toward that vision, yet the unspoken assumptions and ways of doing things that are part of the existing culture continue to exert a powerful influence until they are gradually replaced by new norms that are in keeping with the new shared vision.

Gradually Change the Culture

The sort of culture change we are considering here does not happen overnight. It happens gradually, and it follows rather than precedes the steps that help us attain the cultural shifts we intend. We live into the new shared vision, step by step. We cannot simply tell people that we are changing the parish culture and expect it to happen. In fact, telling people we are changing the culture would likely have little meaning for the average parishioner. As leaders, your insight into the many facets of life in the RCIA and the parish help you to grasp the interdependent practices, attitudes, and assumptions that contribute to the culture of your community. Most parishioners only know the parish through their limited experience of Mass, occasional service or learning opportunities, or social events. This is why establishing urgency and communicating the vision in a compelling way is so crucial. Helping people understand what needs to change and why is a far more effective manner to lead them toward transformation. As we experience the effects of the initial changes in our plan, we also—often without the average parishioner knowing it—begin to experience a change in culture toward a life of discipleship, holiness, and mission. Once begun, we can build on early experience and discern future action in order to move steadily toward the vision we have set before ourselves.

We Need to Talk about This

Action speaks. So do words. Both are necessary. In order to keep the vision of lifelong transformation in people's hearts and minds, we must communicate the vision in every way possible. Communication is not only essential as we bring the vision to people in the early stages of the change process, but rather, we share the vision, why it is important, and the impact of embracing the vision regularly, through homilies, parish print and social media, and in personal interaction. Remember, this is not only about the process of change in the RCIA and the parish. We are also hoping to move people toward an encounter with God's love and deepening commitment to Jesus Christ. The cultural shifts we are exploring will lead to a more evangelizing community.

Leading for Change, Step 8: Anchoring New Approaches in the Culture

Kotter's final step in the change process is to anchor new approaches in the culture (154–166). Doing so ensures that all of your study, reflection, discussion, plans, and new practices will be sustainable in the long term. By firmly embedding the shared vision and resulting practices in the culture, the parish will continue on the journey of lifelong conversion in Christ through changes of pastor, staff, resources, parishioners, and the joys and challenges of circumstances beyond your control. As you no doubt recognize and are likely already experiencing, it will not always be easy. It will, however, be sure to change the RCIA participants and team, the parish, and you as you journey together in common faith and shared joy.

Taking Stock

At this point in your journey of transformation, it will be good to recap the eight steps we have taken or will take to effect change among people, the RCIA process, and in the parish. Look back over your notes at the end of each chapter. Take time to summarize, synthesize, and assess your progress on each of the steps below.

1. Establish a vision

It is crucial that you discern a compelling vision for the RCIA and for the parish in order to foster ongoing conversion in Christ. What is your vision? Why is it urgent? What needs to change in order to bring the vision to life?

2. Create a vision team

It is not possible to lead for change alone. You need a vision team, a guiding coalition, that will embrace the vision, share it with others, and implement steps to make it a reality. Who is part of your vision team? In what ways will they contribute to making your vision reality?

3. Make your vision a reality

It is necessary to have a plan to bring the vision to life. This requires clarity and succinct strategies that will focus attention, energy, and progress. At the end of chapter 3, you developed an initial plan through the Appreciative Inquiry process. You will fine-tune the plan at the end of this chapter as you prepare to make your vision reality.

4. Share your vision

The vision for conversion will only become reality when it is embraced by the community of faith. You, along with members of the vision team and other parish leaders, must share the vision in order for it to become reality. How is this being accomplished now? What future communication (formal and informal) will engage parishioners in the work of ongoing conversion in Christ?

5. Remove barriers to your vision

It is likely that you will meet obstacles along the way as you lead for change. It is important to acknowledge and manage the obstacles, whether they be people who are not yet committed to the vision or structures within the RCIA process or parish that prevent the vision from becoming reality. What barriers have you identified? How are you or the vision team managing the obstacles that could prevent progress toward your vision?

6. Celebrate progress toward your vision

It is important to celebrate progress along the way. Doing so increases momentum and ensures that the long-term vision will come to life. What are the signs of progress toward your vision at present? What markers or indicators of progress will you look for as you continue to bring about your vision for conversion?

7. Keep your vision alive

Even as you celebrate progress toward your vision, you must keep the vision alive in order to bring it about in lasting ways. What structures are in place or are being planned to ensure that the vision comes to life in a lasting and sustainable manner? How will your vision team contribute to the process of keeping the vision alive?

8. Make your vision last

Making the vision last requires a change in parish culture so that the norm for everyone in the community is ongoing conversion in Christ. What signs of the culture of conversion are you perceiving now? How will you lead for long-term change in parish culture in order to bring about your vision for conversion?

It is time to fine-tune your plan and make it reality! Use the table below to succinctly capture your shared vision and the steps necessary to move toward your vision for your people, process, and parish.

	Discover Identify current experience or practice. What is "working"?	**Dream** What is your shared vision? What are your hopes, dreams, and prayers?	**Discern** What practices, behaviors, and norms will bring about the shared vision? What changes are necessary?	**Do** What will be? What steps will you take to bring the vision to life? How will you bring about the practices you have discerned?
People: RCIA participants and team members; parishioners				
Process: The RCIA process as it is enacted in your community				
Parish: The parish, its people, processes, programs, and practices				

Conclusion

I didn't completely understand what I was saying "yes" to when I began my first year of leading the RCIA process. To be truthful, there were many moments in which I wondered if I should have accepted the invitation at all. I felt overwhelmed and inadequate far too often. Yet, there were brief moments in which I glimpsed God's grace in the conversion that was beginning among participants, team members, and parishioners, and those glimpses urged me on.

At first, I thought that we might simply make a few adjustments to the way in which the RCIA process had been enacted in the past and that these minor changes would be sufficient. Very soon, however, I realized that we had to change what we were doing in a much more substantial way. While I could enumerate the elements of the process that were not "working," the prospect of being an agent of change was not something I relished. There were many people and structures within the parish that seemed determined to maintain the status quo. I found myself wanting to minimize the change that was needed in order to pacify those who did not want to change. I was tempted to tell myself and those around me that we could surely muddle through and make the best of what was already in place. Yet, I knew that this is not what we were called to do. Discipleship is not about maintaining the status quo but about challenging anything counter to Christ's message of transforming love.

In the midst of that first year, I also realized that if the RCIA process and the parish were to lead people to accept the call to ongoing conversion, I had to change. I had to grow in my willingness and ability to lead for change. I had to learn to articulate why the changes I suggested were necessary and to draw a group of people together who could bring about the change. I had to think clearly about my own strengths and weaknesses, as well as those of the RCIA and the parish as a community of disciples, in order to advocate for and bring about our vision for conversion. Notice it was "our" vision, not solely mine. While I was the one who initially raised important questions and the need for change, the vision had to be shared. That meant that my personal vision was not always identical to the one discerned by the pastor, vision team, and pastoral council. The shared vision had to be the one toward which we moved. This is part of being in community, of moving from "me" to "we."

I did not know then what I do now and so could not "prove" that the changes I felt were needed would make a real difference. This is one of the reasons why I accepted the invitation to write this book. I hope that it will offer you the encouragement you need in order to be the catalyst for change that your RCIA process and parish need.

Change is scary. Change is hard. It is easy to stick with what we know. And yet, change is necessary. It is also enlivening and transformative. The vision for conversion we have explored may seem outlandish, more than what is possible or perhaps even reasonable in your parish, and yet, imagine for just a moment what might be were the vision to come to pass.

Imagine your vision of conversion coming to life in your RCIA process and in your parish. Think about the hearts that will be touched and the lives that will be transformed as your vision becomes reality. You may meet obstacles and unexpected delays along the way. You are sure to find grace as well. You will experience the joy of the Gospel, alive and active, as people follow Jesus more deeply, grow in holiness, and reach out with Christ's love.

Pope Francis urges us to be bold and creative in our ministry. He said we must "abandon the complacent attitude that says: 'We have always done it this way.' I invite everyone to be bold and creative in this task of rethinking the goals, structures, style and methods of evangelization in their respective communities." Pope Francis urges us to make these changes "generously and courageously, without inhibitions or fear" (Joy of the Gospel, 33).

I also urge you, with the help of the Holy Spirit, to overcome whatever fear or hesitation you might have in making the changes necessary for your RCIA process to become a catalyst for ongoing conversion in your parish. The work that you do in this ministry is profoundly important. If you ever feel discouraged or weak or not up to the task, keep in mind St. Paul's message to the disciples in Corinth:

> [The Lord says] "My grace is sufficient for you, for power is made perfect in weakness." (2 Cor 12:9)

Amen, may it be so! May your vision for conversion come to life within you, your RCIA process, and your parish.

Bibliography

Arrupe, Pedro. *Finding God in All Things: A Marquette Prayer Book*. Milwaukee: Marquette University Press, 2005.

Cooperrider, David, and Diana D. Whitney. *Appreciative Inquiry: A Positive Revolution in Change*. San Francisco: Barrett-Koehler Publishers, 2005. See also http://www.davidcooperrider.com/ai-process/.

"Faith in Flux." Pew Research Center. Forum on Religion & Public Life. http://www.pewforum.org/2009/04/27/faith-in-flux/.

Francis, Pope. The Joy of the Gospel (*Evangelii Gaudium*), Apostolic Exhortation on the Proclamation of the Gospel in Today's World. November 24, 2013.

"Frequently Requested Church Statistics." Center for Applied Research in the Apostolate (CARA). https://cara.georgetown.edu/frequently-requested-church-statistics/.

Gray, Mark M., ed. "How Many Catholic Converts Stay? A Quick Back of the Envelope Reality Check." *Nineteen Sixty-four* (blog). Center for Applied Research in the Apostolate (CARA). http://nineteensixty-four.blogspot.com/2016/02/how-many-catholic-converts-stay-quick.html.

Hilkert, Mary Catherine. *Naming Grace: Preaching and the Sacramental Imagination*. New York: Continuum, 1997.

John Paul II, Pope. At the Beginning of the New Millennium (*Novo Millennio Ineunte*). Apostolic Letter. January 6, 2001.

————. On Catechesis in Our Time (*Catechesi Tradendae*). Apostolic Exhortation. October 16, 1979.

Kotter, John P. *Leading Change*. Boston: Harvard Business Review Press, 2012.

Powell, Kara, Jake Mulder, and Brad Griffin. *Growing Young: Six Essential Strategies to Help Young People Discover and Love Your Church*. Grand Rapids, MI: Baker Books, 2016.

Rite of Christian Initiation of Adults. Study ed. Collegeville, MN: Liturgical Press, 1988.

United States Conference of Catholic Bishops. Co-Workers in the Vineyard of the Lord. Washington, DC: USCCB, 2005.

————. Go and Make Disciples: A National Plan and Strategy for Catholic Evangelization in the United States. Washington, DC: USCCB, 2002.

————. *National Directory for Catechesis*. Washington, DC: USCCB, 2005.

————. *Our Hearts Were Burning Within Us: A Pastoral Plan for Adult Faith Formation in the United States*. Washington, DC: USCCB, 1999.

————. Stewardship: A Disciple's Response. Washington, DC: USCCB, 2002.

Vatican II Council. Constitution on the Sacred Liturgy (*Sacrosanctum Concilium*). December 4, 1963. In Austin Flannery, ed., *Vatican Council II: The Conciliar and Postconciliar Documents*. Collegeville, MN: Liturgical Press, 2014.

————. Dogmatic Constitution on the Church (*Lumen Gentium*). November 21, 1964. In Austin Flannery, ed., *Vatican Council II: The Conciliar and Postconciliar Documents*. Collegeville, MN: Liturgical Press, 2014.

Winseman, Albert L. *Growing an Engaged Church: How to Stop "Doing Church" and Start Being the Church Again*. New York: Gallup Press, 2007.

CPSIA information can be obtained
at www.ICGtesting.com
Printed in the USA
LVHW020412170423
744530LV00021BA/305